Head Trauma

Strategies for
Educational Reintegration

Head Trauma

Strategies for
Educational Reintegration

Second Edition

Joan P. Gerring, M.D.
Medical Director
Pediatric Comprehensive Neurorehabilitation Program
Kennedy Krieger Institute
Assistant Professor of Child Psychiatry and Pediatrics
Johns Hopkins University School of Medicine
Baltimore, Maryland

Joan M. Carney, M.A.
Educational Specialist
Pediatric Comprehensive Neurorehabilitation Program
Kennedy Krieger Institute
Baltimore, Maryland

Singular Publishing Group, Inc.
San Diego, California

Singular Publishing Group, Inc.
4284 41st Street
San Diego, California 92105-1197

Typeset in 11/13 Melior by House Graphics
Printed in the United States of America by McNaughton & Gunn

Library of Congress Cataloging-in-Publication Data

Gerring, Joan P., 1943–
Head trauma: strategies for educational reintegration. – 2nd ed. / Joan
P. Gerring, Joan M. Carney.
    p. cm.
    Rev. ed. of: Head trauma / Christine Duncan Rosen, Joan P.
Gerring. c1986.
    Includes bibliographical references and index.
    ISBN 1-879105-74-8
    1. Brain-damaged children—Education—United States. 2. Brain-
damaged children—Rehabilitation—United States. I. Carney, Joan M.
II. Rosen, Christine Duncan, 1929–   . Head trauma. III.Title.
[DNLM: 1. Brain Injuries—in infancy & childhood. 2. Brain Injuries—
rehabilitation. WS 340 G378h]
LC4596.G47 1992
371.91'6—dc20
DNLM/DLC   92-11621
for Library of Congress   CIP

Contents

Preface vii

Acknowledgments xiii

Chapter 1 Anatomy of the Brain 1

Chapter 2 Early Recovery 7

Chapter 3 Long-term Recovery:
Acute and Postacute Rehabilitation 31

Chapter 4 Implications for School Planning 63

Chapter 5 Reintegration: The Process 81

Chapter 6 Educational Assessment 101

Chapter 7 Instructional Strategies 113

Chapter 8 Summary and Issues 139

Appendix A 149

Appendix B 151

Appendix C 155

References 157

Glossary 165

Subject Index 169

Preface

The decision to revise and rename this text was prompted by several developments that have occurred since *Head Trauma: Educational Reintegration* was published in 1986. First, the widespread usage of Magnetic Resonance Imaging (MRI) has allowed increased resolution of brain areas and frequently demonstrates damaged areas in cases of mild and moderate head injury. Second, this refined neuroimaging procedure to visualize damaged areas has spurred an increased demand for new methods of neuropsychologic assessment and treatment for all intensities of injury. Third, the trend of decreased length of stay in rehabilitation hospitals continues, with an increased focus on postacute school-and-community-based cognitive programs. Fourth, public law has recognized head injury as a handicapping condition in special education, but most school personnel remain untrained in this area. Fifth, greater numbers of head-injured survivors are receiving increased attention, and their need for adequate services must be better addressed. And finally, the authors recognized the need to offer strategies for educators and clinicians to enhance postacute management of the cognitive, behavioral, and emotional deficits following head injury.

Dr. Christine Rosen, the first author of *Head Trauma: Educational Reintegration*, has left the field of head trauma rehabilitation to become an educational administrator. Dr. Joan Gerring, a child and adolescent psychiatrist and currently the medical director of the Kennedy Krieger Rehabilitation Unit, has replaced Dr. Rosen as the first author. Joan Carney, a special educator on the Rehabilitation Unit and a specialist in the field of head injury, has expanded on the information contained in the first text and has contributed recent developments to the body of educational knowledge on head-injured students. Many references have been made to this text since it was published, and the contributions of Dr. Rosen have been invaluable in the construction of this revision.

Each year, 100,000 children younger than 15 years old are admitted to U.S. hospitals with acute head injury (Kraus, Fife, & Conroy, 1987). Some will require long-term assistance from society in the form of special education and medical resources, as well as community support in recreation, socialization, job preparation, and probable lifetime supervision for many activities. Personality, life-style, range of responsibility, career, and social outlook have been drastically altered for these children by a few seconds of inattention or perhaps a misperception of depth. Those who have been suddenly and traumatically injured by falls, assaults, and vehicle-involved accidents provide the impetus for writing this book.

Not all head injuries are severe, and not all severe head injuries result in serious losses. Actually, 5% of children admitted to hospitals with head injury have severe injuries, 3% have moderate injuries, and 93% have mild injuries (Kraus et al., 1987). But for those whose injuries are both severe and lasting, there are many problems to be addressed. These are problems that include availability of adequately trained and informed professionals in patients' local communities and access to resources that offer psychosocial, medical, educational, and vocational support.

Schools are to children what workplaces are to adults. At the time of hospital discharge, however, children will not have recovered to the extent that one would have recovered from other illness or disease. In spite of this, families and educational staff can expect many head-injured children to return to school, albeit with a modified program. Support is essential to assure success at some level. (No one would expect brain-injured adults to return to their former jobs immediately after discharge able to carry out tasks as though uninterrupted.) Allowances need to be tempered with expectations and demands to maintain a balance between expecting too much and expecting enough.

Head-injured children and adolescents will be greatly helped, or hindered, by the responses of adults in the community of schools, churches, temples, YMCA-YWCAs, health centers, and the workplace. Teachers and others in the educational community, however, fill an especially vital role in helping head-injured students move to a status approaching routine and normalcy. School is the most appropriate place for children to gain reassurance that achievement is possible again—even while being confronted with enormous new difficulties in thinking, remembering, speaking, reading, or concentrating.

The following chapters provide information for rehabilitation professionals, school personnel, and families. This book provides details for the following authors' conclusions:

- Public Law 94-142 and its subsequent amendments, particularly Public Law 99-457, which expanded special education services to infants and toddlers, and Public Law 101-476, which defined head injury as a handicapping condition, provide for special education services to children with head injury.
- Although not designed for this purpose, schools become the primary provider of postacute rehabilitation programs for children and adolescents who have sustained head injury.
- Head-injured students are unique in many ways and require the individualized experienced professional assessment and program development afforded to all children with disabilities.
- Methods of special education in use for other handicapping conditions are not always applicable to this population.
- Head-injured students reenter school with deficits from their injury, compounded by extended absence from school, and influenced by their pretraumatic academic functioning.
- The effect of head injury on academic and social reintegration appears to be greater for secondary than for elementary students.

• There are very few educational or recreational summer programs that are appropriate for recently discharged head injury students.

This book addresses the major problems associated with education of these students. Because children who are survivors of severe closed-head injury represent a relatively new population, there are not abundant data to verify the range of outcomes. The literature and findings on adult recovery from head injury and those few studies of child injury that exist offer evidence that effects may differ. What may be true for head-injured adults is not necessarily true for head-injured children and adolescents.

This new population owes its existence to a combination of developments. Over the last two decades, the availability of emergency vehicles and helicopter transport has greatly reduced the time between injury and medical care. Shock trauma units in large, central hospitals are on call with highly developed technology and well-trained personnel ready to administer critical and intensive emergency care. Advances in the education and sophistication of personnel and the development of complex equipment have kept pace with expanding medical understanding about injury, coma, and the recovery process. For these reasons, the acute care of head injury has undergone great strides during the 1970s and the 1980s, resulting in greatly increased patient survival. Many of the patients alive today would not have survived previously. Survival is not without irony, however; many patients are left with severe deficits. Thus, more survive, but they do so at the cost of great compromise across a spectrum of physical and mental abilities, and emerge from hospitals with severe problems that the community of educators, health workers, and families must address.

The discussions and recommendations that follow are based on a literature review and on the authors' experience as members of a pediatric rehabilitation team from September 1981 to March 1992. During this period, the Pediatric Comprehensive Neurorehabilitation Unit of the Kennedy Krieger Institute treated 300 children and adolescents with head injury, aged from infancy to 21; essentially, all of these patients were eligible to return to school. Open-head injuries have become more common since the first book was published, largely because of the increase of gunshot wounds to the head among the younger age group. The total population includes patients with other brain and spinal cord disorders such as encephalitis, stroke, and nervous system tumors. However, the emphasis of this book remains the treatment and rehabilitation of severe closed-head injury. The clinical course and educational experiences of our patients form the bases for the judgments and conclusions reached here, and it is believed that this group is representative of the general population of children and adolescents who have experienced severe closed-head injury. The authors' clinical experience with this increasing population of survivors is now 12 years.

Because brain injury pervades all, the educational problems of severe closed-head-injured students are more likely to be appreciated if discussed in the context of the medical course that has preceded school reintegration rather than in a vacuum. For all those who work with these youngsters, it is important to learn about where they have been and what they have been through. The reader will be brought along a medical journey, of sorts, in preparation for the education and management of these students after they leave the hospital to return to school.

Chapter 1 provides a review of some basics about the anatomy of the brain. Chapter 2 describes the medical treatment for head injury and the various problems that can occur during the early recovery period. The postacute process of cognitive/behavioral/emotional rehabilitation is emphasized in Chapter 3. Chapter 4 provides a discussion of the implications of the sequelae of head injury on educational programming. In Chapter 5 readers are given an outline of the process that will provide optimal school reintegration. Issues of educational evaluation are addressed in Chapter 6, and Chapter 7 follows with a sampling of specific strategies recommended for use with children and adolescents who have sustained head injury. Chapter 8 summarizes some of the issues for families and professionals caring for youngsters with head injury and reviews questions frequently asked by school personnel.

Acknowledgments

To all of the patients and their families whose losses, accomplishments, and frustrations have taught us so much.

To Rob who never complained and was always supportive. To my parents, who believe I can do anything, and to Jill for taking the time to review the manuscript.

To Robert and Judy Gerring for their encouragement and to Donna Gross for her valuable technical assistance.

Chapter 1

Anatomy of the Brain

The brain is the central organ of the nervous system. The nervous system is the organ system of thought and activity, both voluntary and involuntary. The brain and connected spinal cord constitute the central nervous system. The cranial and spinal nerves, along with their associated nerve cell collections called ganglia, comprise the peripheral nervous system. Nerve cells consist of a cell body and one or several fibers, which conduct impulses toward or away from the cell body. Collections of nerve cell bodies are referred to as gray matter because they are gray in appearance. Fiber collections are referred to as white matter because most nerve fibers are encased in a sheath of myelin that is white in color. The central and peripheral nervous systems are in constant communication with one another and the activity of one is always influenced by the activity of the other.

Nerve fiber collections, or tracts, may cross from one side of the central nervous system to the other. Ninety percent of the fibers of the pyramidal tract, a motor tract concerned with extremity motion, cross to the opposite side in the lower brainstem (Clark, 1975). In this fashion, an activity performed on one side of the body may be attributed to neuronal control on the opposite side. When focal injury affects a specific cerebral motor area on the left side, then a motor deficit on the right is generally the result. If the primary motor area controlling hand movement is damaged by a stroke on the left, then the right hand may be paralyzed. From the highest to the lowest levels of the central nervous system, this crossing of fiber tracts keeps both sides of the nervous system interdependent and in constant communication.

The brain consists of two large cerebral hemispheres, the cerebellum and the brainstem. The right and left cerebral hemispheres comprise the largest and uppermost part of the brain and are protectively encased in the skull. The hemispheres control the highest functions of thought, memory, language, sensation, and voluntary movements. Although other animals have cerebral hemispheres, in humans this part of the brain is the most highly developed of any.

A layer of nerve cells called the cortex covers the entire surface of the cerebral hemispheres, giving this portion a gray appearance. White matter, or nerve fibers, underlie this cortical mantle. The surface of the hemispheres is divided into a series of folds, or gyri, next to furrows called sulci, or fissures. Certain of these fissures divide the brain into portions called lobes. The right and left cerebral hemispheres are incompletely divided by the medial longitudinal fissure. At the bottom of the fissure the hemispheres are joined by a broad band of connecting fibers called the corpus callosum.

Each hemisphere is divided into four lobes (Figure 1-1). The frontal lobe lies in front of the central sulcus of Rolando and above the lateral Sylvian fissure. The lateral fissure and the central sulcus are two prominent, easily identified grooves on the lateral cerebral surface. The frontal lobe occupies about the anterior third of the hemisphere. Because of its anterior location, it is vulnerable to injury from pedestrian and/or vehicular trauma. The frontal lobe is the most advanced part of the brain developmentally and contains cells and connections that are not present in lower animals. The frontal lobe consists of the primary motor cortex, the supplementary motor areas, and the prefrontal areas. (Association, projection, and commissural fibers are richly distributed throughout the frontal lobes from where they spread out to connect and interconnect all parts of the central nervous system.) The prefrontal cortex is believed to be essential for the regulation of attention and the performance of executive, social discourse, and interpersonal

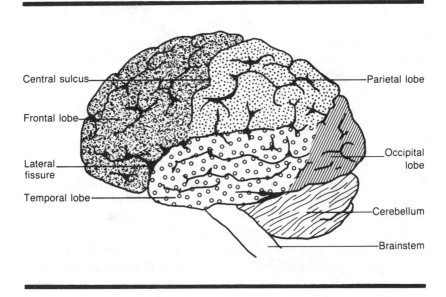

Central sulcus

Frontal lobe

Lateral fissure

Temporal lobe

Parietal lobe

Occipital lobe

Cerebellum

Brainstem

Figure 1-1. Lateral view of the brain.

functions. Executive functions include anticipation, goal selection, planning, monitoring, and efficient processing of information (Stuss & Benson, 1987). Social discourse is the ability to interact productively with others in the form of discussions and conversations (Dennis, 1990).

The temporal lobe occupies the lateral aspect of the cerebral hemisphere and is also particularly susceptible to damage from blunt trauma. The portion of the temporal lobe on the lateral surface of the hemisphere lies in front of the occipital lobe, below the lateral fissure and a line extending posteriorly from the fissure to meet the frontal boundary of the occipital lobe (Crosby, Humphrey, & Lauer, 1962). The temporal lobe contains language, auditory, and memory areas. Damage to the temporal lobe may lead to severe memory deficits, hallucinations, paranoid thinking, and certain types of seizures.

The occipital lobe lies behind a line drawn from the parieto-occipital fissure to the preoccipital notch. The visual cortex and the visual association areas are located here. The parietal lobe extends from the central Rolandic sulcus to the parieto-occipital fissure. Here are located sensory association and projection cortices, as well as speech association areas. Parietal lesions may produce astereognosis, sensory apraxias, and certain kinds of aphasia. (Astereognosis is the inability to recognize an object placed in the hand with the eyes closed. Apraxia is the inability to perform a purposive skilled act, even though the sensory and motor systems are intact.)

There are other important cortical anatomic and functional areas, including the limbic system. This system is believed to be involved in the emotional content of conscious thought processes. The main limbic brain structures are the cingulate gyrus, the anterior thalamic nucleus, the parahippocampal gyrus, the hippocampus, the uncus, and the amygdala.

The brainstem is connected with the cerebral hemispheres at its rostral end and with the spinal cord at its caudal end. The cerebellum is connected to the brainstem on its dorsal surface. The brainstem consists of all the fiber tracts that exit and enter the cerebral hemispheres. Cell collections within the brainstem are the sensory and motor nuclei of the cranial nerves and other nuclei that regulate voluntary and involuntary activities throughout the body.

The brainstem is divided into the medulla, pons, midbrain, and diencephalon. Nuclei in the diencephalon regulate temperature, heart rate, blood pressure, and appetite. The reticular formation, a collection of cells and fibers extending through the medulla, pons, and mesencephalon, is especially important in the regulation of consciousness. The brainstem is a small structure and all of its contents are vital. Any temporary or permanent disturbance to the brainstem can cause widespread neurologic impairment, because multiple structures are in very close proximity throughout its length. Patients with severe brainstem damage with less severely affected cerebral hemispheres sometimes may not be able to speak or move but may remain both responsive and aware. Tumors in the brainstem are often inoperable, as even the most delicate surgical effort will damage important fibers or cells.

The cerebellum is a portion of the brain located under the occipital lobe and attached to the pons, medulla, and midbrain. It maintains muscle tone and equilibrium, and coordinates muscle group movement. The cerebellum also possibly contributes to skilled mental performance by sending signals for carrying out new programs to the frontal association cortex

(Leiner, Leiner, & Dow, 1986). Damage to the cerebellum results in ataxia, impaired balance, and decreased muscle tone.

The neuron, or nerve cell, is the basic unit of the nervous system. It consists of a nerve cell body and cell processes called axons and dendrites. Axons are nerve cell processes that transmit impulses away from the cell body. Dendrites are the nerve processes that transmit impulses toward the cell body. A nerve cell has one axon and one or many dendrites. In the cerebrum and cerebellum, nerve cells are arranged in extensive laminated sheets. Other nerve cell bodies are grouped in cell collections called nuclei or ganglia.

A brain cell in the cerebral gray matter may have processes that extend to a nerve cell in the lower part of the spinal column. The nerve processes of the second neuron travel in a peripheral nerve to a muscle that it innervates. Or the nervous impulse may pass through several neurons as it moves from its origin to the organ that it innervates. Nerve processes also originate in the various organs to transmit messages back to the brain. Nerve circuits are thereby established that provide for a continual interchange of information between the brain and its peripheral connections.

Conduction usually occurs in one direction at the nerve cell synapse. The synapse is the area where the fine processes of one neuron are in contact with the fine processes of another neuron. An impulse travels from dendrite through nerve cell body through axon. At the synapse, a neurotransmitter is released in the form of a vesicle, a fluid-filled pouch enclosed by a membrane, into the synaptic cleft. This vesicle then produces or inhibits an impulse in the dendrites of the adjacent neuron by a process called cell depolarization. In this manner, the impulse travels from cell to cell.

Afferent fibers conduct impulses toward the cell body of the neuron; efferent fibers conduct impulses away from the cell body of the neuron. Nerve fibers in the brain and spinal cord that have a common origin and a common destination are called tracts. The cranial and spinal nerves consist of both afferent and efferent fibers. Efferent nerve fibers transmit impulses from the central nervous system to peripheral organs. Efferent fibers terminate in muscles and glands, and their discharge results in muscle activation or hormone secretion. Afferent nerve fibers transmit sensory impulses from peripheral organs back to the central nervous system.

When the brain is damaged, deficits stem from injury to those areas of the brain that govern the involved functions. The injury by a missile, as in open-head injury, is discrete, and brain areas in the path of injury will be affected with predictable deficits. If a bullet passes through the right frontal motor cortex, then structures on the left side of the body will be paralyzed.

Blunt injury, on the other hand, results in more diffuse brain damage. Primary damage occurs to structures at the point of impact and includes diffuse axonal injury, major vessel tears, and brain lacerations. Damage may also occur at the point opposite the impact point as the brain is pushed against the interior of the skull. This injury at the point opposite is referred to as the contrecoup injury. Secondary injury refers to the low oxygen, high carbon dioxide, low blood pressure, increased intracranial pressure, and seizures that occur as a result of the primary injury (Bruce, 1990). If the right frontal motor cortex is at the point of impact, then a left-sided paralysis or motor weakness may occur. A right-sided or bilateral paralysis, however, may be a consequence of the contrecoup injury or of the more generalized secondary injury.

Diffuse injury to the white matter by mechanical stretching and shearing of nerve fibers at the time of injury is the most common type of abnormality or lesion detected after closed-head injury. Contusion or disruption of the cortex is the second most common abnormality detected by neuroimaging. The lesions in these two areas may or may not be accompanied by bleeding or hemorrhage. Lesions are also commonly noted in gray matter collections underneath the cortex, as well as in the brainstem (Gentry, Godersky, & Thompson, 1988).

Chapter 2

Early Recovery

In casual conversation, the driver of a state of Maryland emergency vehicle explains how medics determine the hospital to which accident victims are rushed. "If they look like teenagers, we bring them to the University of Maryland Shock Trauma Unit; If younger, to Johns Hopkins." Both hospitals maintain shock trauma units designed especially for quick response to severe emergencies. Indeed, acute care of closed-head trauma is best carried out at large, central referral hospitals because only such hospitals have the equipment, personnel, and facilities to provide the necessary high level of care. The speed with which an individual is transported to an intensive care center is a critical step in modifying the pathological chain of events that stem from the initial impact injury. Further, the availability of highly skilled emergency personnel and sophisticated medical equipment profoundly alters the course of recovery and long-term effects of injury.

Consider the substance and texture of the brain and its protective structure, the skull. The brain is the consistency of stiff gelatin. The skull, designed to protect the brain from external, penetrating injury, is a bony, hard shell. Inside the skull are uneven protuberances against which the gelatinous mass is forced during a sudden impact. When a car moving at 60 mph stops suddenly against an abutment, another car, or a tree, the brain's soft mass of gelatinous tissue—also traveling at 60 mph until the impact—slams against the unforgiving, hard, protrusive interior of a passenger's skull, tearing and shearing the tissue internally.

As Kolb and Whishaw (1980) point out, the brain can be seriously injured from a sudden impact or blow to the head whether or not the skull is fractured, and conversely, skull fracture is not necessarily accompanied by brain damage.

IMMEDIATE EMERGENCY PROCEDURES

Neurologic and respiratory status is assessed quickly when accident victims are brought into the emergency room. Medical personnel first determine whether the person's airway is obstructed and if so, they insert a tube into the trachea, or windpipe, to facilitate breathing. (This surgical opening into the trachea is called a tracheostomy.) They also must control bleeding and determine the extent of multiple injuries. Monitoring of all vital signs and pertinent medical functions begins immediately, including systemic and intracranial blood pressure, heart rate, and respiratory rate. Unconscious patients are frequently aided in breathing by respirators that control the quantity of gases that reach the lungs by regulating the depth and duration of breathing. Frequent blood gas analyses measure the amount of oxygen and carbon dioxide in the blood and the pH. All of these parameters are recorded frequently with flow charts that are invaluable in tracking progress or deterioration; the charts also note the effects of multiple medications that are administered. An assessment of neurologic functioning is given in a Glasgow score.

> Glasgow Coma Scale: a measure of the depth and duration of unconsciousness. See page 13 for a longer discussion.

DIAGNOSIS OF INJURY

Two important procedures allow for the rapid localization and definition of abnormalities that are present inside the head or in the skull. The first procedure is a radiology technique that is called Computerized Tomography, or CT scanning. A CT scan is the method of choice for a severely injured patient because it is easy and rapid to perform and because patient movement is not a problem. A CT scan gives important information on edema (swelling) and any presence of blood clots that may have to be removed surgically. Thus, diagnoses of brain pathology can be made within minutes of a patient's entering the hospital. This rapid diagnosis of intracranial bleeding or hematomas (blood collections) is crucial in determining a treatment plan, for there is great danger of excessive blood putting sufficient pressure on brain structures to cause further damage and eventual death. The main role of CT scanning is to separate surgical from nonsurgical cases.

The CT scanner was developed by Hounsfield (1973). This advanced X-ray gives a computerized three-dimensional representation of the contents of the skull. It is an extremely valuable diagnostic tool that is noninvasive (i.e., diagnosis is not dependent on an instrument entering the patient's head). The CT scanner does not identify abnormalities such as epilepsy, but defines types of brain disruption and abnormal masses.

After the first 3 or 4 days of the injury, Magnetic Resonance Imaging, or MRI, becomes the method of choice for patient assessment. MRI scanning reveals more important acute clinical abnormalities and is superior to CT scanning in subacute, chronic, and remote phases of injury. Tissue disruptions, white matter injury, and hematomas are clearly demonstrated with MRI (Figure 2-1). MRI is also superior to CT scanning in the evaluation of patients with mild and moderate head injuries (Kelly et al., 1988). MRI abnormalities can be demonstrated in up to 90% of scans performed after mild and moderate head injuries (Levin et al., 1987).

Magnetic Resonance Imaging (MRI), introduced in 1982, is a sensitive neuroimaging procedure to detect abnormalities of brain tissue. This imaging technique does not depend on radiation exposure, but rather on the magnetic properties of tissues. A computer image reconstruction displays excellent contrast among different brain components. MRI images of the posterior parts of the brain and spinal cord have particular value, because bone often interferes with other types of imaging techniques. Caution has to be paid, however, by patients and personnel involved in MRI, because MRI machines produce a high magnetic field which can pull any object made of iron-like material toward the magnet, which can lead to personal injury and scanner damage (Zimmerman & Bilaniuk, 1989).

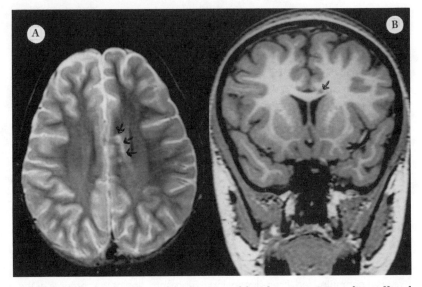

Figure 2-1. A. Axial MRI image of 5-year-old girl patient S.R., who suffered severe closed-head injury followed by 2 days of coma. MRI taken 2 months after injury demonstrates white matter axonal injury in the corpus callosum (arrows). **B**. Coronal MRI image of patient S.R. demonstrates axonal injury in the left corpus callosum (arrow).

IMMEDIATE EFFECTS OF INJURY: INTRACRANIAL PRESSURE AND EDEMA

The brain often swells after injury because the injury causes an increased amount of blood to flow to the brain. Edema fluid, increased water from the blood vessels and from inside the cells, contributes to the swelling (Bruce, 1990). If the rise in intracranial pressure and the accumulation of edema fluid are not controlled, the patient runs an increased risk of death, for there is no place for release in the confines of the skull. If the swelling is extreme, the brain outgrows the cranial cavity and moves outward and downward in a process called *herniation*. This process may damage the centers of breathing and circulatory regulation in the brainstem and result in death. (See Figure 2-2.)

Edema: Excessive accumulation of fluid within cells or in tissue spaces. The fluid in tissue spaces leaks from the damaged blood vessels and consists of a clear liquid portion of the blood.

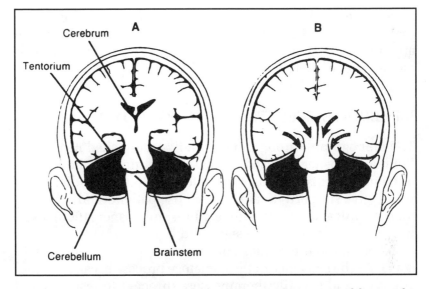

Figure 2-2. Central transtentorial herniation. **A** shows normal brain relationships in a coronal section. The tentorium is a tough connective tissue membrane separating the cerebral hemispheres from the cerebellum. **B**. As a result of traumatic brain swelling, the cerebral hemispheres expand to compress and displace brainstem structures. This pressure and displacement of vital brainstem areas lead to pathologic circulatory and respiratory changes that may terminate in death. Modified from Plum and Posner, 1987. Reprinted with permission.

The emergency management of closed-head injury consists of treatments to control acute brain swelling and intracranial pressure. A variety of mechanical means and drug treatments are used to decrease cerebral blood flow, reduce and remove edema fluid, and lower intracranial pressure. General measures include elevation of the head, control of hypertension with medication, and provision of adequate oxygen. Specific measures include the use of diuretics to reduce elevated intracranial pressure and the use of high doses of barbiturates to lower cerebral metabolism, thereby putting the patient in a hibernation-like state (Lehman, 1990). Raised intracranial pressure (ICP) is much more likely when the initial Glasgow Coma Scale is low (3 or 4). Eighty percent of a series of 35 children with Glasgow scores of 3 or 4 had elevations of intracranial pressure with the pressure rise occurring between the first and fifth post-injury days (Bruce et al., 1979). The intracranial pressure may remain elevated for several days. Elevated levels of intracranial pressure and reduction in blood flow result in decreased amounts of oxygen to tissues, resulting in focal tissue impairment (Bruce, 1983).

IMMEDIATE EFFECTS OF INJURY: COMA

The monograph *Stupor and Coma*, first published in 1966 by Plum and Posner, focused increased attention on the process of coma, or unconsciousness. Before 1966, the medical staff would give supportive care to comatose patients and then wait for the clinical course to evolve. Plum and Posner (1966) urged physicians to observe eye signs and breathing patterns of the comatose patient for clues concerning depth and duration of coma. As the sequence of the comatose process became clearer, attention and specific therapy were directed for each step of the process.

Patients who suffer severe closed-head injury become comatose or unconscious for brief to very long periods of time. A comatose patient does not respond to the stimulus of voice, but lacking other complications, continues to have breathing and blood circulation. However, faculties indicative of a thinking being are suspended, and the patient does not communicate through sounds or movement with caregivers. When the patient moves eyes or limbs in response to a voice command, it is an indication that the coma has ended. Most commonly, the end of coma is defined as the patient's attainment of the ability to respond to simple commands (Ommaya, 1966). The command may be as simple as a request to raise a designated finger. Eye opening may precede the termination of coma by many days and muteness may continue for a number of days after the simple command response is attained.

Recovery From Coma

Patients emerge from coma gradually. The longer the coma, the more lengthy the process of emergence. Responses to simple commands, at first inconsistent, become more predictable. Gradually, patients obey more complicated commands. The return of speech is the next landmark, but the onset of speaking may be delayed if there is oral motor pathology or a complication surrounding a tracheostomy.

Injury Severity

Severity is best measured by the patient's initial Glasgow Coma Scale score (GCS), measured at the injury site or on arrival at the hospital. (See Appendix A.) Glasgow Coma Scale scores of 8 or less out of a possible score of 15 indicate severe head injury. Moderate head injury is defined as an admission GCS of 9 (9/15) to 12 (12/15) with no further deterioration or an admission GCS of 13 to 15 with an abnormal radioimaging procedure necessitating brain surgery. Most other injuries are mild with initial GCSs of 13 to 15. Employing the GCS of 13 to 15 to indicate mild head injury replaces the use of the term concussion, which can mean momentary unconsciousness or up to an hour of unconsciousness. Using similar definitions of severity, an epidemiologic study over a 1-year period in California noted 5% of pediatric head injuries to be severe, 3% to be moderate and 93% to be mild. The study showed 3% of the patients died before arrival at the hospital, and 3% died in the hospital (Kraus et al., 1987).

Glasgow Coma Scale: In 1974, Teasdale and Jennett utilized the accumulated knowledge about coma to devise a short, easily administered scale to measure the depth and duration of unconsciousness. Intensive care personnel can use this scale as a rough indicator of a patient's progress in the intensive care setting. It consists of three components: measures of eye opening, motor ability, and verbal ability. The three measures are added and a patient receives a score of from 3 to 15. The score is often given as a numerator with the denominator of 15, the highest possible score, e.g., 3/15, 4/15, etc. Patients who have initial scores of 8 or less are usually admitted to intensive care units. Patients with scores greater than 8 are admitted to a neurology or neurosurgical unit where care is not as concentrated or as intense.

IMMEDIATE EFFECTS OF INJURY: OUTCOME MEASURES

The Duration of Coma

Duration of coma, duration of posttraumatic amnesia, and the initial Glasgow Coma Scale score constitute the most important outcome indicators in closed-head injury. Coma lasting longer than 7 days results in some degree of permanent impairment. Coma lengths between 7 and 90 days have variable outcomes, depending on the type and location of injury. Long-term neuropsychologic and behavioral impairments are commonly noted after these injuries. Comas of 90 days or longer invariably result in multiple handicaps — physical, neuropsychologic, and behavioral. In a series of 20 children and adolescents who regained consciousness after 90 days, 11 had the ability to communicate, 5 ambulated independently, and 4 had IQ recoveries to the range of 70 or above (Kriel, Krach, & Sheehan, 1988).

The Duration of Posttraumatic Amnesia

Three kinds of amnesia, or periods of time with no conscious memory, are associated with head injury. A patient with *retrograde amnesia* has no memory of the time prior to the injury, whether or not the injury was followed by a period of coma. A patient with no recollection of the time following the injury and coma suffers from *anterograde amnesia*. Retrograde amnesia tends to decrease with time and has not been useful as a prognostic indicator. The duration of retrograde amnesia, most often shorter than anterograde amnesia, is usually measured in minutes or hours.

Russell, working with a series of 200 closed-head injury patients, defined the third kind of amnesia associated with head injury, *posttraumatic amnesia* (PTA), as the period after trauma when the patient is not storing continuous memories (Russell, 1932). PTA includes anterograde amnesia and the length of coma, if it has occurred. Patients are not consistently oriented during this period of time, although they may appear oriented at any one testing. Sometimes they appear to be confused. They may carry on simple conversations and give correct answers to questions, or execute activities without noticeable change in their regular manner of performance.

Medical personnel have long determined the duration of PTA by asking patients (at any time following emergence from amnesia) when they "woke up" or "came to themselves" (Russell, 1932). Years after injury, people retain a reasonable memory of how long their PTA lasted. By contrast, years after injury, it is often difficult to retrieve records that give an accurate measure of the patient's length of coma. PTA is useful as a measure even in very short durations of coma, including momentary lapses of consciousness. Under such circumstances the concept of PTA helps explain why a patient who had a few minutes of unconsciousness and a few days of PTA is unable to work for several months. The duration of PTA has prognostic importance regarding outcome. In Guthkelch's study (1979) of 398 head injury cases, it was 6 months before the majority of patients with a PTA lasting between 1 and 7 days had returned to work. Also, Lishman (1968) noted that patients with longer PTAs had a higher incidence of psychiatric deficits. A prospective study of head injured children and adolescents showed a relationship between permanent IQ deficit and PTAs of at least two weeks (Chadwick, Rutter, Brown, Shaffer, & Traub, 1981). In cases of minor injuries, the duration of PTA is in direct relation to the duration of postconcussion symptoms (Guthkelch, 1979).

Standard measures beyond the patient's report of "waking up" have been developed to measure the termination of PTA. These measures include the Galveston Orientation and Amnesia Test (GOAT) and the Children's Orientation and Amnesia Test (COAT). (See Appendix B.) Posttraumatic amnesia ends when the patient is oriented consistently and continuous memory is restored. The duration of PTA may be determined by repeated testing of orientation and memory. In the case of R.S. below, sequential GOATs were administered to document the termination of her PTA.

Case History

R.S. is a 16 year old 12th grade female student who suffered severe closed head injury as a driver in an auto accident. Her initial Glasgow score was 8/15 and her CT scan was within normal limits. She was hospitalized in a neurointensive care unit and was comatose for 9 days. The patient was admitted to the rehabilitation hospital on the 22nd day after her injury. The termination of PTA was documented by sequential GOATs and occurred 36 days after injury. During the PTA, R.S. answered "I don't know" to the question "What is the first event you can remember after the injury?" After the PTA ended, she answered, "Waking up at JFK . . . I thought it was a dream." Deficits in short term memory persisted after the termination of the PTA.

Galveston Orientation and Amnesia Test (GOAT): A 10-item bedside test of orientation and memory that is administered serially to document the return of continuous memory (Levin, O'Donnell, & Grossman, 1979). This test has been adapted for use with children and is called the Children's Orientation and Amnesia Test (COAT). See Appendix B (Ewing-Cobbs, Levin, Fletcher, Miner, & Eisenberg, 1990). When patients have achieved a certain score on sequential COAT or GOAT testing, they are no longer considered to be in PTA.

The Initial Glasgow Coma Scale Score

The initial Glasgow Coma Scale score is a third outcome indicator in closed-head injury. In the 1981 year-long San Diego County epidemiologic study of pediatric head injury, the rate of moderate or severe disability, persistent vegetative state, or death was 100% with a GCS of 3 or 4 on admission and 65% with a GCS of 5 to 8 (Kraus et al., 1987).

The Age Factor

Age at injury is an important factor in regard to general outcome, children 6 years of age and older having better cognitive, motor, and brain recovery than younger patients (Kriel, Krach, & Panser, 1989). Studies of cognitive outcome suggest that younger children have a poorer outcome than older children; the outcome being worst in the first 2 years of life. In one study of severely head-injured children, those children injured after the age of 10 had longer periods of coma but higher posttraumatic IQs than children injured prior to age 10 (Brink, Garrett, Hale, Woo-Sam, & Nickel, 1970). Another group studied children who had depressed skull fractures followed by coma at least 2 years previously. The prevalence of reading disorder in this sample was significantly higher in children who had been unconscious longer and who had been injured before the age of 9 (Shaffer, Bijur, Chadwick, & Rutter, 1981).

IMMEDIATE EFFECTS OF INJURY: SEIZURES

Seizures are a common complication of severe head injury. The seizure disorder occuring after head injury is called posttraumatic epilepsy. Injury to the brain causes a disturbance in the electrical rhythms that, in turn, provokes an abnormal electrical discharge. The chances that these seizures will occur with closed-head injury are 5%. The seizure incidence is higher with open head injury. Even minor head injury may result in an immediate seizure in some children. As the severity of injury increases, however, the incidence of seizures rises. Brink, Imbus, and Woo-Sam (1980) describe a 32% incidence of seizures in a group of patients with a median duration of coma of 5 to 6 weeks.

Seizure disorders may take a variety of forms. Seizures may be convulsive, involving motor movements, or nonconvulsive in nature. Nonconvulsive seizures are the more common disorders and include simple partial and complex partial varieties. When seizures consist completely of mental symptoms, such as fear or depression, they are often difficult to recognize. Simple partial seizures are not usually accompanied by a loss of consciousness. These seizures involve a discharge in one or another area (e.g., movement of an extremity, an abnormal sensation of smell or taste, a hallucination, or the experience of anger). Complex partial seizures may sometimes begin with simple partial symptoms, but are usually accompanied by impaired consciousness (e.g., mild confusion, a haze that comes and goes, or a tendency to stare). Complex partial seizures last about 30 seconds to 3 minutes (Murray, 1985).

Immediately after trauma, the electroencephalogram (EEG) often demonstrates a variety of abnormalities, including diffuse or focal slow rhythms. As the distance from trauma lengthens over weeks or months, the EEG often appears more normal. Many patients will eventually have a pattern that is interpreted as normal even though posttraumatic epilepsy may appear later.

Electroencephalogram (EEG): A measure of electrical activity of the brain, picked up by a standard placement of electrodes on the scalp. Deviation from the usual recorded rhythms over certain brain areas is defined as pathological. Abnormalities include excessively slow or fast activity and certain spike and wave patterns. The EEG may be unremarkable, however, in the presence of brain damage, or may show abnormalities when the patient has no signs or symptoms of illness.

Posttraumatic seizures may occur early in the first week following trauma or appear much later. The more severe the trauma the greater the likelihood of early seizures. When early posttraumatic seizures are present, children are at risk for eventual development of late posttraumatic seizures as well. A more severe injury also increases risk for late seizures that may make their appearance years afterward. However, 90% of posttraumatic seizures occur within the first 2 years after trauma (Bruce, 1990). Less obvious seizures may appear as a deterioration in the recovery process. A previously attentive child, for example, may appear disinterested or inattentive if there are numerous seizure discharges unaccompanied by abnormal movements. Although seizures will cease in one-half of the patients who develop posttraumatic epilepsy, one-quarter to one-third of patients will continue to have 10 to 15 seizures a year (Rosman & Oppenheimer, 1982). These seizures are often difficult to treat.

The standard treatment of seizures is with medication, but helping a child attain good seizure control requires finding a delicate balance between the drug dosage and the side effects. All children and adolescents who have had seizures must be followed on a regular basis by a physician. The physician is helped in this by drug assays for which a therapeutic range of blood levels is specified. Toxic effects may appear either when the medication surpasses the therapeutic range or even while it still is in the therapeutic range. Common side effects of special concern for the child and adolescent population are sedation and hyperactivity. These behavioral effects may seriously impede classroom performance; indeed, it is often teachers who notice these symptoms. In addition, teachers are in a position to monitor the occurrence of seizures and the behavioral effects of any changes in medication.

The prophylactic use of antiseizure medicine may be effective in the prevention of early posttraumatic seizures that occur in the first week after trauma (Temkin et al., 1990). However, the prophylactic use of antiseizure medicine has failed to prevent the development of epilepsy in injured humans (Willmore,1990).

IMMEDIATE EFFECTS OF INJURY: PHYSICAL PROBLEMS

Many severe medical problems occur along with the head injury, including injury to internal organs necessitating surgery, fractures, massive infections, hypertension, and hormone system derangements. More than 50% of a large series of pediatric head-injured patients admitted to trauma centers had extracranial injuries, injuries of moderate-to-extreme severity not affecting the head or neck. Children with extracranial injuries are more severely involved and have more residual impairments than children who just have head injuries. Children injured in traffic-related accidents, which tend to occur in older children, are more likely to have head injuries plus extracranial injuries (Di Scala, Osberg, Gans, Chin, & Grant, 1991).

Motor Impairment

Diffuse cerebral and brainstem injury results in damage to pathways that regulate movement, posture, and coordination. Spasticity appears early after injury and presents a combination of increased muscle tone and exaggerated neuromuscular reflexes that results in limited movement of the affected limbs. It may affect 1, 2, 3, or 4 limbs, but it most commonly affects one (hemiparesis) or both sides (quadriparesis) of the body. Although the paretic side is usually the side opposite the injury, it is not always so — most severe closed-head injury results in more than one area of brain damage and can involve both sides of the brain.

Patients enter physical therapy early in the intensive care course to prevent muscle contracture, or tightening, in both upper and lower extremities. When patients are unable to move by themselves, they are positioned and provided with passive exercises to the limbs to prevent motor decline. Other effects of motor impairment are detailed in Chapter 3.

Sensory Impairment

A variety of visual symptoms may be evident after head injury, reflecting damage to the eye itself, the cranial nerves governing vision and ocular movements, the optic chiasm, the optic tracts, the occipital cortex, and the vessels supplying these areas. Blunt injury can cause blindness through disruption of the optic nerves or chiasm or by direct injury to the occipital cortex, but permanent loss of vision is unusual (Bruce, 1990). Loss of vision in a portion of the visual field (visual field defect or field cut) results from damage to structures along the visual pathway, from the optic nerve to the occipital cortex. Homonymous hemianopia, one type of visual field defect, is blindness in one-half of each field of vision. Cranial nerve damage may lead to signs and symptoms that include unequal pupillary size, drooping of the upper eyelid, strabismus, blurred vision, and double vision. The time course of these symptoms is variable.

Hearing and balance are mediated by a common set of structures in the central nervous system. Significant damage to any of these structures in the brainstem, cerebellum, or cortex may lead to hearing loss and/or vertigo, a position regulation disturbance resulting in dizziness and a sensation of whirling. Many symptoms of auditory and vestibular impairment are persistent, including some types of sensorineural hearing loss (Healy, 1982).

Defects of smell have been documented in 72 of 1,000 adults with severe head injury (Leigh, 1943). In 12 of these cases, there was a perversion of smell perception, termed parosmia. Recovery of olfactory function was noted in 6 of the 72 cases and was usually seen within 6 months of the injury.

Internal Injuries

Internal injuries incurred at the time of the head injury have long-lasting effects and may involve any organ. Damage to the spleen may require its removal, which, in turn, makes patients especially vulnerable to infection. Other organs or parts of organs, such as the lungs, liver, kidneys, or bowel, can be so damaged that their present or future function is compromised. A lung or bowel segment or an entire kidney may have to be removed if damaged, if the blood supply is threatened, or if bleeding is excessive.

Fractures

Fractures are the most common extracranial injury. Facial fractures occur most often, but fractures of the clavicle, ribs, pelvis, and long bones of the arms and legs are also frequently seen. A fracture may be a severe complication. For example, adult patients with traumatic pelvic fractures have a 10 to 25% mortality, mainly from hemorrhage (Soderstrom, 1982). Fractures may hinder or lengthen the rehabilitation process, because treatment may require restriction of mobility for an extended period. Wiring of the jaw to treat a mandibular fracture prevents the patient from speaking and may impede initial progress in speech/language rehabilitation. Long bone fractures may be treated by traction or casting, forms of immobilization that may impede early ambulation. However, the duration of immobilization is reduced by use of lightweight casts that permit ambulation and by internal and external fixation devices that allow patients to be out of bed and to walk as soon as possible after surgery.

Hypertension

Hypertension is another medical problem that is commonly seen after severe head injury. This complication was seen in 20% of the patients in the Brink series (Brink et al., 1980). The blood pressure returns to normal levels as part of the recovery process, but the pressure elevation may be prolonged. Several medications are useful in the control of this type of blood pressure elevation, including nifedipine, clonidine, enalapril, and propranolol.

IMMEDIATE EFFECTS OF INJURY: NEUROPSYCHIATRIC PROBLEMS OF RECOVERY

There is wide variation in the way that patients act, feel, and behave during the period of posttraumatic amnesia. They may be calm and quiet or they may be agitated and noisy. Also, periods of calm may alternate with periods of agitation. If the patient traverses PTA in a calm state, he or she will not interfere with caregiving and will need no behavioral intervention. If, however, the patient becomes fearful, disruptive, or aggressive, then medical personnel will refer the patient for psychiatric assessment and management. Patients receive a psychiatric diagnosis only if they pose a danger to themselves or others as they awaken from their comatose state. The pathologic behaviors occurring during PTA are collectively termed Delirı the DSM III-R psychiatric manual (American Psychiatric ɔociation, 1987). The following behaviors may occur during ɔhe delirious state.

DSM III-R - Diagnostic and Statistical Manual of Mental Disorders, 3rd Edition, Revised. The current psychiatric diagnostic manual of behavioral and emotional disorders. Operational criteria for diagnosis are listed for all entries. Representative diagnostic sections include anxiety disorders, substance use disorders, and mood disorders. One chapter is devoted to organic mental disorders. Another describes diagnoses seen in infancy, childhood, and adolescence. The manual is used in all psychiatric facilities and by many other health professionals. A further revision is scheduled for 1993.

Sleeping and Waking Patterns

An impaired sleep–wake cycle is common during emergence from coma and the period of PTA. Periods of alert wakefulness alternate with periods of sleep during the 24-hour day. Resumption of a more normal sleep-wake cycle with increasing hours of sleep during the night is a positive sign of recovery. However, the need for daytime naps and increased daytime sleepiness may persist long after termination of the PTA.

All impediments to nighttime sleep should be removed from the surroundings of such an individual. A small light should be left on in the patient's room to assist in orientation and to decrease nighttime fearfulness. If possible, a person the patient is comfortable with should remain nearby. Only occasionally will short-term medication be necessary until the sleep–wake cycle returns to normal.

Inattention

Rapid shifting of attention and inability to maintain attention is the hallmark of the delirious state. The patient attends to one stimulus, then quickly turns to another. Therefore, it is difficult to engage such a patient in a task for any length of time. It is also reasonable that misperceptions would be common with these rapid shifts of attention. In the extreme, inattentive patients move rapidly and aimlessly from one activity or location to another. This type of constant activity may be dangerous, as the patient is often indiscriminate about what he or she is doing. This activity is exasperating and tiring to the caretakers.

Inattention that is apparent only on close observation or questioning is no problem during PTA. The passage of time will eventually lead to an increased ability to attend. However, if the shifts in attention are rapid and frequent, then the patient's safety is a primary consideration. The patient will usually not respond to behavioral reinforcement techniques, but instead needs frequent redirection within an environment that is orienting and structured. Medication has limited usefulness, but can be used to slow the person, if necessary.

Illusions and Hallucinations

Illusions and hallucinations may result from continued brain dysfunction during early recovery. These abnormal perceptions may involve any sense. An illusion is a misinterpretation of a real sensory experience. For example, the mistaking of a car screech for a scream is an auditory illusion. A hallucination is the perception of an object when no corresponding real object exists. A vision of a deceased relative is an example of a visual hallucination. Hallucinations of hearing, touch, and smell also occur.

These abnormal perceptions may be frightening, neutral, or comforting. A frightening hallucination, such as the voice of the devil, may prompt a child to try to escape and possibly to hurt him- or herself in the process. On the other hand, voices of a deity or an angel encouraging the recovery of the child, may be comforting and calming. As these abnormal perceptions are short lived and confined to the period of PTA, they do not have a negative meaning in respect to outcome. As a consequence, they are predominantly treated by orienting the patient and clarifying his or her perceptual distortions. More aggressive management is considered when the patient might harm him- or herself or others as a response to frightening illusions or hallucinations. Medications may be used briefly and are usually effective in eliminating hallucinations that occur during PTA.

Activity Levels

A wide range of activity levels occurs during early recovery from head injury. This range is probably related to the location, nature, and extent of injury; the pretraumatic psychiatric condition; and the medications that are used during the acute care course. The patient may remain inactive during PTA, may be normally active, or may show degrees of activity ranging from overactivity to agitation to aggression. Agitation is excess motor activity with the additional component of apparent inner tension. A frequently seen pattern after severe injury is one of short periods of agitation alternating with periods of quiet or sleep occurring regularly over a 24-hour period. The activity level during PTA after mild and moderate injuries has not been well studied.

When the patient is emerging from coma and confined to bed, periodic overactivity manifests itself in a number of ways. The patient may rapidly and randomly move about the bed and can easily slide or fall off. He or she may repeatedly rub one extremity against the sheets, causing an abrasion. Or he or she may occasionally pull out the feeding tube by random arm movements. These time-limited motor problems are managed by positioning, temporary restraint of the extremity, or by other pragmatic mechanical solutions (e.g., a low bed). Sedation is reserved only for extreme, frequent, or long-standing agitation when mechanical treatment has proved ineffective.

Further along in the recovery course, the disoriented ambulatory child may be overly active in a random and impulsive manner. This activity may be continual during waking hours. Such a child can come to harm if this time-limited activity is not controlled. Again, a behavioral solution is the preferred treatment. A trained parent or attendant stays with the child to redirect activity and to gently help focus attention. A structured environment is provided with limited objects and activities so that over-stimulation is avoided. Medication is sometimes necessary to reduce very high and dangerous activity levels. A medicine such as thioridazine or haloperidol may be used in low doses for short periods of time to avoid negative effects on emerging cognitive abilities.

A small percentage of children and adolescents demonstrates aggressive behavior during PTA. Multiple precipitants of aggression include requests to comply (the aggression is an act of impulsive resistance to the request), frightening illusions (the aggression is a fearful response to a perceived intruder), and command hallucinations (the aggression is a response to a command telling the patient to hurt someone).

Behavioral methods are the first line of treatment of aggression. The patient is treated in a nonstimulating environment where he or she is frequently oriented and perceptions are clarified. Reinforcement methods are used to lessen and eliminate aggressive behaviors. In addition, medication is often necessary when behavioral control is incomplete. As no medicine successfully treats aggressive behavior in all patients, a number of medicines must often be systematically tried in order to find an effective medicine for a specific patient. Medications that have demonstrated usefulness in the treatment of aggressive behaviors include lithium, propranolol, and carbamazepine.

Sometimes aggressive patients may be transferred to behavioral or psychiatric units for management. This decision is dictated by the severity of the behavior and the ability of the rehabilitation staff to work with behaviorally disordered patients. T.H. is an adolescent who suffered severe closed-head injury and was transferred from a rehabilitation to a psychiatry unit because of severe aggressive behavior. Clinical experience indicates that patients who demonstrate aggressive behavior early during their recovery period often have a premorbid history of aggressive behavior.

Case History

T.H. is an 18-year-old white male who suffered closed-head injury with a brainstem and a right hemispheric contusion as an automobile passenger in March 1982. The patient had been hospitalized for a head injury and a brief period of unconsciousness at age 6. Migraine headaches were diagnosed at age 9. T.H. was a poor student with problems starting in the third grade, including aggression and disruptive behavior. Truancy, drinking, and drug abuse became problems in high school. The patient quit high school on his 18th birthday. The patient had been placed on probation three times in connection with the destruction of property. T.H. was unconscious for 5 days. Four days after coma ended, aggressive behavior began. He developed a posttraumatic seizure disorder in the 2nd week after injury and was admitted to a rehabilitation hospital 2 months after injury. The patient was verbally and physically aggressive toward staff members. He forcefully threw a glass pestle across his room, threw a chair at the wall, and hit his nurse in the abdomen. He made several attempts to escape from the hospital. In one attempt, the patient put his leg over a rail on a second floor porch. Thioridazine was used to achieve mild sedation, with a mild decrease in the level of aggression. Because T.H. was a behavioral/ psychiatric patient, with limited need for other disciplines, transfer to a psychiatric unit was arranged.

IMMEDIATE EFFECTS OF INJURY: FAMILY RESPONSES

Psychosocial Responses

The sudden onset of a severe illness such as closed-head trauma is a great crisis to each family. The possibility of death may exist for several days, and the family lives with this uncertainty. It struggles to maintain its integrity and well-being, despite grief, fear, and anger that are sometimes overwhelming. For several weeks, family life is centered on the crisis. Job schedules are disrupted. Sleep is caught at irregular times. Parents may be troubled by anxiety dreams. Eating is sporadic and the nutrition quality often falls for family members. Most families have had no preparation for the medical system of advanced technology that they now enter with their child. In a few days' time they are asked to assimilate such terms as CT scan, tracheostomy, and respirator so that they can begin to ask important questions concerning management.

Siblings are often in the care of nearby relatives. Depending on their age and the family dynamics, they may or may not actively participate in events. However, the lives of siblings living with the patient will be affected by the events of the accident and its aftermath. Because of the magnitude and com- plexity of tasks addressed by the parents, the questions and needs of siblings are often ignored for a time.

Families show different styles of adaptation to crisis. There is little research concerning an optimal family background for coping with crisis, but several contributing factors for adaptation have emerged from observation and work with the families of patients at the Kennedy Krieger Institute:

- **Stable family background.** A follow-up study by Gilchrist and Wilkinson (1979) found a stable family to be a positive influence on the prognosis of 84 head-injured adults.
- **Family style.** Family style is characterized by the family's

interaction with the outside world and may be exaggerated during a crisis. Some families work well with outside helpers and establish a mutual give-and-take relationship. Others are untrusting and isolated and find it difficult to surrender the care of their children to others. Very dependent families rely heavily on staff guidance and are unable to initiate needed services by themselves.

- **Family support.** Psychologic resources are necessary to embark on the long and trying period of rehabilitation. Families who lack resources or who have been unable to resolve lesser crises in the past are placed under severe strain and risk deterioration. Social work support is an important adjunct for these families during the inpatient and outpatient periods of recovery.

Families with a strong religious belief find powerful and long-sustaining support from this belief during their crisis. In the long run, those families who persevere, continue to hope, and are part of a cohesive support system, maintain themselves best through the difficult rehabilitation period.

Emotional Responses

Anger and denial are two common early emotional responses to the injury. Anger, open or suppressed, arises from the incomprehensible nature of the occurrence and the resulting distress of the entire family. Obtaining a lawyer to investigate the circumstances of the accident and initiating litigation are socially acceptable mechanisms for the discharge of angry feelings. Anger can also be focused on medical treatments or personnel. Some parents develop conflicts with particular staff members over various treatment methods. Other parents will focus on an aspect of the hospital environment that they find troublesome. One mother became concerned that her child would further injure herself when agitated by hitting herself against the sides of her metal bed. The mother spent several weeks making padded cloth bedliners until she felt satisfied that one was effective. Staff members must analyze each expression of parental dissatisfaction to separate the real and present issues from the diffuse and projected responses stemming from feelings about the accident.

Families frequently deny the severity of the injury as explained by medical or rehabilitation staff. For example, families of patients who have experienced many weeks of coma and who continue to show severe resultant handicaps will talk about college attendance as an imminent occurrence. Attempts to dissuade such families are futile. Sometimes family denial seriously interferes with rehabilitation. Parents may relate to the child as if there were no handicap and make no attempt to contribute to or support the treatment effort. For example, such parents may not cooperate with treatment suggestions when they take their child out of the hospital on a therapeutic weekend pass.

Such denial frequently lessens as the time from injury lengthens. Although parents may continue to maintain that their child will recover without handicap, most increasingly subscribe to treatment recommendations. In such instances, initial denial may be viewed as a protection against the severe psychologic stress. With time, most families gain some mastery of their new situation and no longer have to use denial to keep severe tension under control.

Other emotions are prominent in different individuals. Depression and anxiety may appear in family members who have a predisposition toward those conditions. Most often, the appearance and resolution of strong feelings are managed within the family with assistance and support of friends, neighbors, and religious community. When the emotional reaction of parents negatively affects a child's treatment, or if parents are unable to reduce levels of tension with the help of their own social network, then intervention is offered. Hospital personnel, mindful that personality traits tend to be temporarily exaggerated during crises, do not suggest counseling or therapy until a reasonable estimate can be made of the persistence of maladaptive patterns of behavior. When families are isolated, or when there is severe family dysfunction, early intervention in the form of crisis management is usually attempted by the social work or psychiatric staff.

Posttraumatic Stress Disorder

Patients and their families are vulnerable to the development of a posttraumatic stress disorder. This mental disorder occurs as a response to events that cause extraordinary stress in most people. It is an extraordinary stress to experience or to witness severe bodily injury. If the injury results in prolonged coma accompanied by retrograde amnesia, then the patient usually has no recollections surrounding the trauma and is not at risk for the development of posttraumatic stress disorder (PTSD). With less severe injuries, where there is recollection of the injury, the child or adolescent can develop this disorder. All witnesses or participants, however, are at risk for posttraumatic stress disorder.

There are three kinds of symptoms that occur with this disorder. The first is the reexperience of the event in some fashion, either by nightmare, through a flashback, or by repetitively playing out certain aspects of the event. The second is persistent avoidance of stimuli associated with the trauma. The person avoids any thoughts, feelings, or activities that would lead one to recollect the trauma. He or she may also develop a feeling of detachment from other people. The third is increased arousal, manifest as difficulty falling asleep, angry outbursts, or being hypervigilant. These symptoms usually appear soon after the trauma, but are sometimes delayed.

PTSD is treated with psychotherapy alone or with a combination of psychotherapy and medication. During the therapy, the psychiatrist alternately supports and confronts the symptoms of PTSD to help the patient tolerate and better understand the thoughts and emotions connected with the stressful event. The goal is to help the patient develop adaptive means of responding to these painful thoughts and emotions. The choice of medication is determined by the particular symptom or symptoms that need to be addressed (Gerring & McCarthy, 1988). J.B. is a teenager who suffered mild head injury, and had recollections of the traumatic event.

Case History

J.B. is a 14-year-old white female who sustained a brief loss of consciousness as an unbelted passenger in an auto accident. She was alert and oriented to time, place, and person on her arrival in the emergency room. She returned to school the next day, but symptoms of tiredness, confusion, difficulty in concentrating, and headaches prompted an admission to the hospital 2 weeks later. CT scan and MRI were performed with unremarkable results. Continuing distress 9 months after her injury prompted a comprehensive rehabilitation evaluation. The patient described periodic flashbacks of the accident, a withdrawal from her circle of friends, interrupted and restless sleep, difficulty concentrating, and hypersensitivity to sound. J.B. no longer wanted to learn to drive and she made great efforts to avoid passing the accident scene. Her parents described her mood as solemn, saying that she rarely appeared happy. She also was more irritable and angry toward them than before the accident. Recent memory and word-finding impairment were detected on neuropsychological testing. Diagnostic impressions were PTSD and postconcussion syndrome. Psychotherapy was initiated to help J.B. work through and lessen the painful emotions she had been experiencing, to understand the changes that had taken place in her, and to adjust to these changes by setting more reasonable expectations for herself. Cognitive strategies were introduced into her school program to minimize her impairments in recent memory and word finding.

SUMMARY

The time period from severe head injury to the end of posttraumatic amnesia is packed with events and emotional reactions to these events. This period is measured in weeks and months. Advanced technology ensures the survival of most patients who arrive at the intensive care unit. As the comatose condition subsides, rehabilitation efforts are directed toward the deficits that become apparent. Each rehabilitation specialist periodically assesses the pattern of recovery and the prominent deficits in his or her area of interest. As soon as the patient has the mental capacity to incorporate new material, these specialists institute treatment strategies. At the termination of posttraumatic amnesia, patients with severe injury have received a complete assessment of deficits, and have embarked on comprehensive programs for their alleviation. Patients who have suffered mild and moderate head injuries often reenter their community and school without the benefit of assessment and therapy, and may manifest neuropsychologic and psychiatric impairments that make reentry a difficult process.

Chapter 3

Long-Term Recovery: Acute and Postacute Rehabilitation

It is common for patients to be still comatose and in post-traumatic amnesia when they leave the acute-care hospital. At that time, patients are no longer on respirators and can breathe on their own (although some continue with tracheostomies), and they no longer hover between life and death. Much medical and nursing care is still needed, but that care can be given at a less costly and less extensively monitored setting than an acute-care hospital. Rehabilitation care has already commenced at this early stage of recovery, with physical therapists, occupational therapists, and speech language pathologists attending to reemerging abilities.

Rehabilitation medicine, or physiatry, is the specialty that aims to lessen the effects of disability and handicap. Physiatrists help patients improve their ability and performance and work with patients to decrease the disadvantages produced by their injury or disease (Johnston & Lewis, 1991). When the head-injured patient leaves the acute care hospital, he or she may enter a rehabilitation program to facilitate recovery. Depending on clinical condition, the patient will be referred to either an acute or a postacute program.

Seriously head-injured children and adolescents often enter an *acute in-patient program*, the first type of rehabilitation program. On entry into this program, the patient may still have many medical and neurologic problems that need careful attention. In addition to receiving high-intensity medical care, the patient is assessed and treated by rehabilitation specialists in physical therapy, occupational therapy, speech-language pathology, special education, social work, and other disciplines. The patient receives therapies that address the specific goals agreed on by these rehabilitation specialists. The average length of stay in adult hospital-based programs in the United States is 53 days (Cope, Cole, Hall, & Barkan, 1991b).

The average number of days in acute rehabilitation hospital programs has been declining, as patients are more quickly referred for *postacute rehabilitation* care, the second major type of rehabilitation program. There are three main reasons for this shift. First, patients are more likely to be compliant and motivated to perform in real world settings outside of the hospital. Second, patients have improved ability to generalize treatment goals when they are learning in their natural environment. And third, outpatient programs are far less costly on a daily basis because high inpatient hospital costs are avoided (Cope, Cole, Hall, & Barkan, 1991a).

Adult postacute or community reentry programs provide multiple rehabilitation therapies in a variety of settings, including home, community, day treatment, and residential settings. The therapies vary according to the specific program and individual need, and include behavioral management counseling; speech and language services; and social, educational, and vocational skills training (Cope et al., 1991a). As patients' needs change, they move within the same program or from one program to another. The overall coordination of a patient's program is under the direction of a case manager, who is an advocate for the patient and who guides him or her through the different aspects of the system.

In the case of many head-injured children and adolescents, it is a comprehensive special education school program that constitutes the postacute rehabilitation. The school may be the sole provider of postacute services, or it may contract with community agencies to provide some of the needed services. Children who have suffered mild and moderate head injuries will reenter school directly from the acute-care hospital and will then need to be assessed and to enter a treatment program, if necessary. As inpatient rehabilitation stays get shorter, many children and adolescents return to school during an active phase of recovery, often with pronounced remaining disabilities.

Most of the spontaneous active motor and sensory recovery from head-injury is complete by 1 year after the injury. However, there appears to be an extended recovery period for neuro-psychologic and psychiatric deficits that may extend to several years following the trauma. These deficits constitute the major disability for head-injury survivors and are the main barrier to resumption of a normal life. Although the current thinking extends postacute rehabilitation to several years in order to address these neuropsychologic/psychiatric deficits, the optimum length of treatment for the best outcome has not been defined (Cope et al., 1991a).

The long-term follow-up of severely head-injured adult patients indicates a decrease in the level of independence and in employment status from pretraumatic levels. In addition, the incidence of psychiatric problems, behavioral and emotional, increases with time after the injury (Cope et al., 1991a). The treatment of the neuropsychologic/psychiatric deficits of head injury is referred to as *cognitive rehabilitation*.

The long-term functional outcome of severely head-injured adult patients is positively influenced by postacute rehabilitation programs. Adult head-injured patients make significant advances in levels of independent living and vocational and social productive activity as a result of participation in these programs. These functional outcome measures aim to measure the generalizability and persistence of treatment effects in the real world environment (Brooks, 1991). On the other hand, cognitive outcome, as measured by neuropsychologic test results, has not been impressive (Thompson & Filley, 1989).

Postacute rehabilitation care for adults occurs mainly in the private sector in rehabilitation systems created by for-profit providers. These systems include multiple treatment options and attend to patients' needs at all stages of care, from entry to discharge planning to community reintegration. As patients improve or as they develop different needs, they move within the system from one program to another, for example, from a residential behavioral program to a day-treatment program to a community-based home program (Brooks, 1991; Cope et al., 1991a).

Postacute rehabilitation care for most children and adolescents occurs within the public sector in the special education setting. Severely head-injured youngsters may need more services than are customarily assigned for learning disabled children. Head-injured children in special education placements are entitled to receive comprehensive rehabilitation services that include occupational therapy, physical therapy, and speech-language therapy. Severely injured children who have received acute rehabilitation may need prolonged services for multiple handicaps. Children who are less handicapped will need fewer services. Many children with mild and moderate injuries will not receive inpatient rehabilitation, but will later be evaluated as outpatients and then receive therapies in school.

The school system needs to provide the same treatment options that adults receive in the private sector. Well-equipped school systems are capable of providing head-injured students with all the services they need. Many school systems, however, need to contract or work in conjunction with outside agencies to provide the services they cannot provide. As the provision of these multiple services is costly, it is important for the school system to explore various methods of financing such as third-party insurance payments.

ACUTE INPATIENT REHABILITATION

Patients enter acute inpatient rehabilitation programs when they are medically stable and no longer need to be in an intensive medical setting. However, many of these patients continue to be very sick. They may still be comatose or just emerging from coma and dependent in all their care needs. These patients may have periods of great restlessness, along with abnormal sleep patterns. Some patients have complicated fractures treated with immobilizing traction or cumbersome external devices. Other patients have fevers or high blood pressure which need to be monitored and managed. Yet other patients are talking and walking, but continue to be disoriented and easily distractible. The initial assessment of the rehabilitation team takes into account the variable clinical picture of these patients. The team needs to fashion individual programs to fit immediate patient needs.

Most severely head-injured children and adolescents currently enter acute inpatient rehabilitation programs prior to the end of their posttraumatic amnesia in a disoriented state unable to incorporate continuous memories. The benefit of rehabilitation therapies during this early recovery period has been debated. Learning is severely impaired during PTA. But some studies suggest that certain tasks may be learned while the patient is still in PTA. Such patients are unable to acquire and retain verbal information such as word lists and recent events, which are examples of declarative or data-based memories. However, patients may have some ability to acquire and retain certain motor skills, such as performance on a mirror reading task, which is an example of procedural or rule-based memory (Ewert, Levin, Watson, & Kalisky, 1989). Other research demonstrated a reduced and predominantly passive mode of learning information during PTA when testing memory for spatial location (Gasquoine, 1991).

At the end of posttraumatic amnesia, which may be hours for mild head injuries or days to months for severe injuries, patients are consistently oriented to person, place, and date and are able to store long-term memories. It is then that productive rehabilitation begins. The rate of spontaneous recovery in physical and sensory areas is greatest in the year following injury. Rehabilitation specialists have an opportunity to provide aggressive treatment during a period of rapid improvement and change from the end of PTA until the end of the year following injury.

The Interdisciplinary Team

Acute inpatient rehabilitation is conducted by an interdisciplinary team under the medical direction of a physiatrist, a psychiatrist, or a neurologist. Initially, persistent medical problems receive primary attention, but as the patient's physical condition improves, the emphasis shifts from physical rehabilitation to cognitive rehabilitation. As the length of stay in adult inpatient rehabilitation has shrunk from an average of 93 to 53 days in the past decade, early attention is also given to definition and organization of the postacute rehabilitation care. This focus on continuum of care strives to provide the most beneficial therapies over time and to help the patient and his or her family negotiate a complicated health care system.

The child or adolescent receives a thorough assessment on his or her entry to an inpatient program. The youngster is evaluated by members of the rehabilitation team and by other consultants during a 3- to 5-day period. Depending on the clinical condition, this assessment may have to be adjusted as to its content or duration. For example, an extremely agitated patient may need to be evaluated during very brief periods of observation extending over several days rather than in a formal testing situation. At the completion of the assessment, the rehabilitation team members meet in a steering conference to present their results and to decide on the goals and objectives of the admission, the length of the admission, and the type and amount of therapies that will be provided. Generic discharge goals are translated into specific working objectives by the treating disciplines. The 13 generic discharge goals of the Kennedy Krieger Institute Rehabilitation Unit are listed in Table 3-1. Initial objectives decided at the steering conference are extended, achieved, canceled, or replaced by other objectives during the course of the admission. Discussion of the patient's progress and adjustment of objectives are discussed at weekly team conferences. The results of the steering conference are discussed with the family and their approval is sought for the treatment plan. Family input is also important when treatment changes are considered and when discharge planning is taking place.

The inpatient team includes many disciplines. As the goals and objectives of the admission shift, varying team members play primary roles. Physicians and nurses concentrate on medical recovery. The neuropsychologist assesses and monitors cognitive/neuropsychologic functioning. The audiologist assesses and monitors auditory functioning. The nutritionist attends to the diet and the texture of the patient's intake. The physical and occupational therapists focus on the preservation and improvement of extremity function. Cognitive rehabilitation services are assessed and provided by the speech-language pathologist, the occupational therapist, the therapeutic recreation specialist, the social worker, and the special educator. The psychiatrist and the behavioral psychologist diagnose and

Table 3-1. Generic Discharge Goals

1. Patient will achieve medical stability.
2. A safe, effective means of nutrition will be established for the patient.
3. Patient will have functional means of communication.
4. Patient will reach cognitive potential.
5. Referrals will be made to appropriate community and educational resources.
6. Patient will perform activities of daily living (with or without assistive devices) commensurate with motor/cognitive levels.
7. Patient will achieve fine motor skills commensurate with cognitive/motor levels.
8. A program will be established to prevent further physical deformity.
9. Patient will achieve a means of mobility (with or without assistive devices).
10. Patient will adjust to his or her condition commensurate with handicaps and premorbid vulnerabilities.
11. Patient will demonstrate participation in appropriate leisure activities.
12. Patient's caregiver will demonstrate understanding of patient's condition and ability to meet patient's needs.
13. Patient will cooperate in the rehabilitation program and demonstrate appropriate conduct in the discharge environment.

treat the emotional and behavioral deficits that follow head injury. Each therapist treats present needs and anticipates necessary postacute services.

The case manager, or care coordinator, is the team member assigned to coordinate delivery of services to the individual patient. The case manager, usually a nurse or a social worker, is familiar with all aspects of inpatient and outpatient care. This team member ascertains that all assessments are completed and that treatment goals are fulfilled prior to discharge. The inpatient case manager is active in discharge planning and either continues the coordination role in the postacute phase or transfers the role to a postacute case manager. At all phases, he or she communicates medical information to the family and advises them on matters of care.

When the child arrives for inpatient rehabilitation, the special educator contacts the child's school to find out about previous school performance and behavior. The school is continually informed about the child's condition by the special educator, who relays copies of assessments and progress reports. School personnel are invited to visit with the child, to observe the patient during therapies, and to attend progress and dis-charge planning meetings. When coma ends and the child is sufficiently attentive, the youngster is assessed and placed in an educational program. The special educator and the hospital teacher collaborate to define educational deficits and to provide remedial strategies. Before the child is discharged, the special educator participates in school disposition and planning meetings. Along with other team members, the special educator often gives inservice presentations to assist in school man-agement after the child's discharge.

MEDICAL PROBLEMS IN ACUTE REHABILITATION

When the head-injured child enters the inpatient rehabilitation hospital, his or her medical and surgical problems often persist. Some problems are secondary to the head injury and others are secondary to other injuries suffered in the accident. These medical and surgical problems initially may be the primary focus of treatment, with rehabilitation therapies taking a back seat until the patient is medically stable. Many of these prob-lems, such as internal injuries, fractures, and hypertension, span the intensive care and acute rehabilitation periods, and have been discussed in Chapter 2 (Early Recovery). On discharge from inpatient rehabilitation, the patient is referred back to his or her local pediatrician for outpatient management with only occasional consultation from the rehabilitation hospital.

Tracheostomy

Fifty-five percent of 344 severely head-injured children and adolescents in one series had a tracheostomy for airway prob-lems (Brink et al., 1980). This procedure is undertaken when the patient is unable to attain a sufficient quantity of oxygen to the lungs for a prolonged period of time. The decision to perform a tracheostomy is a serious one, for tracheostomy care is detailed and difficult. Fastidious care, including the use of monitoring equipment, must be taken to ensure that the patient's airway remains open and that the delivery of gases is unimpeded. When the patient's clinical condition improves, attempts are made to close the tracheostomy opening gradually so that the patient can resume breathing in the normal manner. The tube is intermittently plugged and progressively smaller tubes are used until the tube is finally removed. The opening into the throat eventually closes, leaving a scar. Occasionally a patient unable to tolerate the withdrawal of oxygen or the closing of the tracheostomy will continue to be tracheostomy-dependent for an indeterminate length of time after inpatient discharge.

Dysphagia

Seriously injured patients frequently demonstrate uncoordinated chewing or swallowing, termed dysphagia, during their recovery. Because of lack of muscle coordination, there is a risk that the ingested food or liquid will pass from the mouth to the pharynx and then inadvertently into the trachea and lungs instead of into the esophagus. An indication that food or drink is passing from the pharynx into the trachea is the appearance of a cough after the patient swallows. The presence of food in the lungs can lead to pneumonia. Because of this danger, patients in early recovery from head injury, many of them comatose or emerging from coma, are fed by a tube from the mouth or nose into the esophagus, thus obviating the need to swallow food or drink. As muscular coordination improves and the patient demonstrates that he or she can swallow and accept pureed food without coughing, a radiologic procedure is scheduled to view the patient's swallowing when given a variety of solid and liquid textures. A recovering patient often demonstrates the ability to swallow solid foods effectively, but the ability to swallow thin liquids often lags. In this case, oral feedings will be instituted with thickened liquids, until the patient can swallow thin liquids without coughing or aspirating liquid into the trachea.

By discharge from the rehabilitation hospital, most patients are able to ingest both solid foods and thin liquids. Prolonged dysphagia is an impairment that is usually seen with evidence of other severe disability. This situation usually requires substitution of oral feedings with the use of a feeding gastrostomy tube.

Scarring

Lacerations, or cuts, and skin abrasions, or scrapes, of many sizes and locations are common after head injury. Healing occasionally leaves disfiguring scars that may have negative psychologic impact. A tracheostomy site may also leave a prominent scar. The plastic surgeon is consulted early to participate in the management of these skin complications.

MOTOR IMPAIRMENT

Motor function is frequently impaired as a result of severe head injury. The most common motor abnormalities are spasticity, ataxia, and a combination of these two deficits. In a series of 344 severely head-injured children and adolescents, 38% of the patients were spastic, 8% ataxic, and 39% both spastic and ataxic at the 1-year follow-up (Brink et al., 1980). Although the vast majority of children who regain consciousness are eventually able to walk, walking is the single most frequently impaired function in the entire group of head-injured children admitted to trauma centers (Di Scala et al., 1991).

Spasticity

Spasticity is an increase in magnitude of the deep tendon stretch reflexes and an increase in muscle tone. Head injury, because of damage to nerve cells and fibers, may result in spasticity of one, two, three, or four extremities, the spasticity usually being more pronounced on one side. Mild spasticity is registered merely as an increase in deep tendon reflexes. Moderate and severe spasticity negatively affect the performance of fine motor movements of the extremities and the quality of the gait. In the most severe spasticity, only gross, nonfunctional movements of the extremities are possible (Brink et al., 1970).

Ataxia

Ataxia results from damage to the cerebellum and to the sensory tracts that regulate coordination of movement. Characteristics of ataxia are impaired balance, intention tremors (shaking movements that intensify with activity and disappear during sleep), and dysarthic speech. Mild ataxia is demonstrated by impaired performance of finger-to-nose, heel-to-shin, and rapid alternating movement tests, but does not interfere with the performance of most motor activities. Moderate and severe ataxia exist when the intention tremor interferes with simple tasks, or when balance is so poor that walking is impaired. An ataxic gait has a staggering quality and is occasionally misinterpreted as drunkenness; a former patient from the Kennedy Krieger Institute was arrested after a minor motor vehicle accident because police believed the youth was intoxicated. Ataxic or dysarthric speech has a scanning, slurred quality. Ataxia was seen in 60% of the 52 patients followed by Brink and colleagues, but the majority of these patients were affected to a minimum degree (Brink et al., 1970).

Treatment of Motor Deficits

Physical and occupational therapists treat the motor deficits following severe head injury. Physical therapists work with lower extremity impairment and are concerned with attainment of ambulation. (See Figure 3-1.) Occupational therapists work with the upper extremities to maximize functional skills of grooming, eating, food preparation, etc. (See Figure 3-2.) Occupational therapists also foster visual–motor and visual–perceptual skills and work with dysphagic patients on feeding and swallowing deficits.

Motor rehabilitation begins early. Physical and occupational therapists in the acute care hospital administer range of motion exercises to comatose patients to prevent muscles from becoming tight and contracted. Plastic splints are constructed and applied to spastic limbs to prevent contractures. Splints continue to be used as long as spasticity continues to be a problem, though their use may be limited to night hours after the child leaves the hospital. Sometimes serial casting of the leg may be used to reduce tone (resistance to passive movement of the muscles), to increase the range of motion, and to prevent shortening of the muscles that cross the ankle joint (Barnard et al., 1984).

A recent study showed 78% of 4,870 children in a series admitted to trauma centers after head injury were discharged

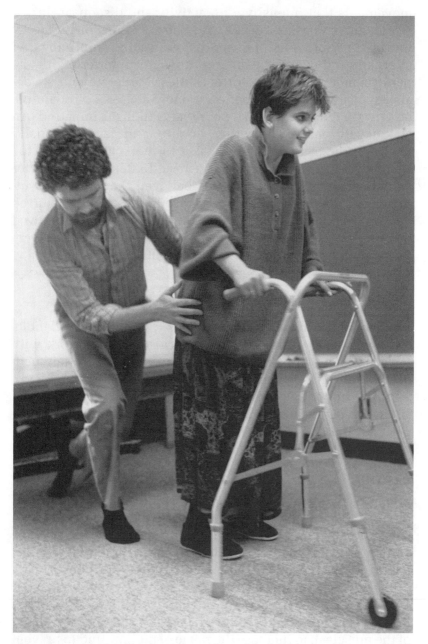

Figure 3-1. The physical therapist assists a head-injured teenager to stand and walk alone.

Figure 3-2. The occupational therapist facilitates fine motor and play skills with preschool head-injured children.

from the acute care hospital without residual impairments. Of the 22% of those patients with one or more impairments, the most frequently impaired motor functions (in order of incidence) were: walking, bathing, dressing, and self-feeding. Walking was the most frequently impaired function, present in 55% of children with one to three impairments and in 94% of children with four or more impairments (Di Scala et al., 1991).

Motor rehabilitation is a major focus in the inpatient acute rehabilitation hospital. Admitted patients receive a complete motor assessment as part of a comprehensive interdisciplinary evaluation. At the completion of the assessment, long- and short-term motor goals are defined in collaboration with the other treating disciplines.

Immobile patients are exercised and splinted, while receiving therapies to reduce overall tone. Patients awakening from coma participate in active and passive exercises of the neck, trunk, and extremities. With further recovery and improvement in cognitive abilities, the patient begins to participate in such functional activities as bathing, grooming, and eating. The occupational therapist or speech-language pathologist assesses chewing and swallowing impairments, initiates exercises to promote a more normal swallowing function, and provides adaptive feeding equipment to ensure optimal oral feeding (Emick-Herring & Wood, 1990).

The physical therapist assesses the patient's potential for ambulation and constructs a graduated program of exercises leading to ambulation — first with assistive devices, such as walkers or canes, and then independently. Plastic orthotic devices may be necessary to stabilize the ankle and/or the knee, to facilitate walking, and to allow for more functional ambulation. In addition to spasticity, other motor abnormalities, such as ataxia, tremors, and neglect of an extremity, impede progress in motor rehabilitation and need to be addressed by physical and occupational therapists working with the head-injured patient.

At the completion of his or her inpatient rehabilitation course, the head-injured patient will have made progress in motor abilities. In a study of 50 adults with a median inpatient stay of 69 days and a mean length of stay of 75 days, most patients were able to move in bed, achieve and maintain sitting balance, transfer from one position to another, achieve and maintain standing, and walk on level surfaces. However, fewer than half of the patients could climb stairs independently (Talmage & Collins, 1983). If it is accepted that spontaneous motor and sensory recovery continue to the end of the first year postinjury, then progress can be expected to continue in the postacute program.

Physical and occupational therapists continue to work with the patient to improve functional motor and sensory skills in the community setting. Motor deficits include impaired timing and sequencing of muscle contractions, as well as poor equilibrium responses and motor behavior during standing and gait. Sensory deficits include a loss of ability to assess laterality and direction, in addition to motor impersistence and perseveration. The therapist assists the patient to relearn functional motor skills by helping him or her to understand the sequence of steps, to perform proper posture and movement patterns, and to practice an activity until it becomes automatic (Rinehart, 1983).

COGNITIVE IMPAIRMENT

General Intellectual Impairment

General intellectual function, as measured by standard tests of intelligence, is impaired after severe closed-head injury. The cognitive level is lowest immediately after injury, but usually recovers quickly in the first few months, and then continues at a slower rate during the rest of the first postinjury year. Intelligence scores continue to improve during the second year, but more slowly. There is a dose-response relationship between the duration of coma or the posttraumatic amnesia and the level of intellectual impairment (Chadwick et al., 1981). In the 1970 Brink et al. series, coma duration of children in the normal range of intelligence was 1.7 weeks, in the borderline range (70-84 IQ) 3 weeks, in the mild mental retardation range (55-69 IQ) 8 weeks, and in the severe retardation range (25-39 IQ) 11 weeks.

Children who survive prolonged unconsciousness longer than 90 days invariably have severe cognitive deficits. In a series of 26 children followed for at least 2 years, four children had functional cognitive recoveries with IQs from 72 to 81. Seven of the children had IQs ranging from 22 to 51, and the remaining 15 were unable to communicate (Kriel et al., 1988).

Neuropsychological testing

The components of cognition are scrutinized in neuropsychological testing. The IQ may return to a pretrauma level after head injury, but the patient may exhibit specific cognitive deficits that represent major disability and prevent normal functioning. The neuropsychologist tests such cognitive components as attention, concentration, memory, motor speed, visuospatial ability, and visuomotor ability.

A distinguishing characteristic of closed-head injury is diffuseness of the injury, with the focal nature of the injury being a distinguishing characteristic of open-head injury. Consequently, the earliest emphasis in neuropsychologic studies of closed-head injury was on the diffuseness of injury and on the definition of random deficits affecting multiple aspects of cognition. In contrast, the emphasis in studies of open-head injury was on the correlation of injury location with specific deficits.

As survival from closed-head injury skyrocketed in the 1970s, neuropsychologists constructed many new instruments to define cognitive deficits. There were two major changes in the 1980s. First, neuropsychologists could work with extensive accumulated data on the incidence of the most common deficits after closed-head injury. Second, the ability of neuroimaging procedures to detect brain abnormalities increased greatly with the introduction of Magnetic Resonance Imaging (MRI) in 1982. After the first few days following injury, the MRI is the most sensitive technique to detect brain abnormalities (Zimmerman & Bilaniuk, 1989). In a 1987 neuroimaging study comparing CT and MRI in closed-head injury patients, 85% of the patients had abnormalities that were visualized by MRI but were undetected by CT; the 85% included both patients for whom CT showed no abnormalities and patients for whom MRI revealed abnormalities in addition to those found on CT (Levin et al., 1987).

As a result, neuropsychologists in the 1990s are shifting their emphasis to define and catalog deficits according to location. Because most closed-head injuries occur to the frontal and temporal lobes, it is not surprising that recent efforts have focused on the definition of neuropsychologic deficits related to these areas. A formidable new problem is the correlation of specific deficits with the multiple areas of involvement frequently demonstrated by the MRI scan.

The neuropsychologist is a central member of the inpatient interdisciplinary rehabilitation team. This specialist defines the patients' deficits and monitors the neuropsychologic changes that occur during recovery. The neuropsychologist ensures that therapists treat the patient according to the patient's current cognitive level. That is, if a 10-year-old child is functioning at a 5-year old's cognitive level, then the treating therapists need to instruct the child with methods appropriate to the younger mental age. Further, he or she helps to construct cognitive strategies to assist therapists in carrying out their work. For example, the neuropsychologist may work with the special educator to devise memory aids for a head-injured student with a severe memory deficit.

Before discharge from inpatient rehabilitation, the neuropsychologist performs comprehensive discharge testing to define the cognitive level and to assist in appropriate outpatient placement. Neuropsychologists in postacute rehabilitation programs monitor patient progress, help determine when a patient is ready to move from one component of a treatment program to another, and consult on individual patient and program treatment strategies.

Patterns of Neuropsychologic Deficits

There are several neuropsychologic deficits that occur commonly after closed-head injury, the appearance and intensity of each deficit being influenced by the type and location of the injury. With severe injury, persistent neuropsychologic deficits correlate with late MRI abnormalities, detected on scans taken 5 to 18 months after injury. Ventricular enlargement on MRI scanning, consistent with a diffuse loss of brain tissue, is particularly associated with persistent poor neuropsychologic performance (Wilson et al., 1988). In an open-head injury, the nature of the deficits is easier to predict from knowledge of the pathway and eventual location of the missile.

Neuropsychological deficits occur after mild-and-moderate injury, although these deficits tend to be less severe and to last a shorter period of time. With mild-and-moderate injury, improvement in neuropsychologic performance has been demonstrated to parallel a reduction in size of the abnormality visualized on MRI scan (Levin et al., 1987). In the Rimel, Giordani, Barth, and Jane study (1982), the major predictors of disability after minor head injury were premorbid characteristics of age, education, and socioeconomic status, while all predictors in moderate head injury were measures of injury severity, for example, coma duration and CT diagnosis.

Memory function is frequently depressed after closed-head injury in children and adolescents. Many types of memory are impaired on neuropsychologic testing, including verbal recall, visuospatial recall, visual continuous recognition memory, and consistent retrieval from long-term storage. In one 10-year follow-up study, nearly 25% of a head-injured child population continued to manifest verbal memory deficits (Gaidolfi & Vignolo, 1980). Persistent memory loss contributes significantly to disability, and memory deficits seriously impede academic, vocational, and social interactions. Students may be unable to remember material from lectures or a homework assignment. Employees may find it difficult to remember sequences in the performance of a job assignment. A social relationship may be disrupted when an important promise is not remembered. C.E. is a patient whose persistent severe memory deficit posed a limitation to viable employment.

Case History

C.E. is a 23-year-old white male who suffered severe closed-head injury as an auto passenger at age 19. Initial CT scan revealed diffuse cerebral swelling. The patient was comatose for 5 days. C.E. demonstrated deficits in rote sequential auditory memory skills at the completion of a 2-month rehabilitation program. He performed at the first grade level on a test requiring literal recall and inferential reasoning about orally presented stories. After discharge, the patient sought employment in retail sales. Being likable and sociable, the patient obtained employment easily. Once employed, C.E. experienced difficulty in remembering schedules, locations of items, and instructions from his supervisor. He has lost several jobs because of this deficit.

Slowness of motor speed, reaction time, speech, and thought are other deficits that may persist. Patients often describe slowed thinking. Decreased speed of information processing has been demonstrated in adult patients (Gronwall & Sampson, 1974). Such slowness hinders verbal and written performance. Students are unable to copy classroom assignments at the speed necessary to keep up with the class. They are reluctant to speak because a single sentence may take two or three times longer to say. This reluctance extends to social conversations as well, as individuals risk being cut off or ignored by people who are unsympathetic or impatient.

Visuoperceptual and somatosensory deficits may persist and lead to disability. The long-term recovery of these functions has not been examined. Visuoperceptual function refers to a person's visual interpretation of shapes, sizes, distances, and locations of objects in the environment. The Bender Gestalt Test, for example, evaluates visuoperceptual ability in the copying of nine geometric figures (Bender, 1938). Deviations from the presented figures demonstrate visuoperceptual deficits. Somatosensory function refers to abilities of the sensory organs to assist in definition and localization of input. A test of graphesthetic ability may be used to evaluate somatosensory function. While the patient's eyes are closed, the examiner traces numbers onto the patient's palm. The patient is asked to indicate the correct number. Failure to give the correct number is an indication of loss of graphesthetic ability.

Other affected neuropsychologic functions include attention, concentration, motor speed, fine motor coordination, visuomotor skills, visuospatial skills, and verbal fluency. These impairments are usually short-term after mild-and-moderate injuries, lasting perhaps as long as a year. Impairment after severe injury is more likely to be persistent, with slow improvement occurring for up to several years.

Frontal Lobe Neuropsychology

The frontal lobes and their subcortical connections, including the basal ganglia, are associated with self-regulation and executive functioning. Self-regulation refers to the initiating, sustaining, modulating, and inhibiting of attention. Executive functions include anticipation, goal selection, planning, and organizing of information (Stuss & Benson, 1987). During performance of these functions, the frontal anterior part of the brain exerts control over the posterior information processing areas of the brain involved in language, memory, and spatial ability. Self-regulation and executive functions are more difficult to test than information processing functions because the structure and organization of the testing situation compensate for deficits in these areas of cognition (Denckla, 1989).

Because the frontal lobe is frequently injured in closed-head injury, neuropsychologists include instruments that assess self-regulation and executive functions in their assessment batteries. Developmental issues also have to be considered when testing children, as self-regulation and executive functions mature from childhood until adult life. Because of these issues, testing of frontal lobe functions is still not well established.

Several instruments may be used to assess frontal lobe neuropsychologic functioning in children. The Wisconsin Card Sorting Test assesses executive functions, with testing of both verbal and visuospatial abilities (Heaton, 1981). Norms for children are available (Chelune & Baer, 1986). The Tower of Hanoi is another instrument that assesses executive functions. This visuospatial planning task has been modified for children and adolescents (Welsh, Pennington, & Grossier, 1991). The Minnesota Computerized Assessment tests self-regulatory function (Greenberg, 1988). It is a continuous performance, or vigilance, task using nonverbal visual targets and providing measures of correct target responses, omissions, commissions, mean response time, and variability of response time. The Controlled Oral Word Association Test assesses verbal fluency. Low scores indicate frontal lobe damage, particularly of the left frontal lobe (Lezak, 1982).

SPEECH-LANGUAGE IMPAIRMENT

Speech-language abilities are frequently affected by severe closed-head injury. Speech and language may be affected by severe open-head injury if brain areas that subsume speech and language abilities are injured. Speech-language deficits following closed-head injury are commonly a combination of specific language deficits and deficits of language utilization and therefore appear dissimilar from the primarily specific deficits that occur after open-head injury. Speech-language deficits also occur after mild-and-moderate head injury, but their nature and temporal course have not been well clarified.

Language Recovery

After severe head injury, patients usually have an immediate loss of consciousness. They may be mute, may say words that indicate they are confused, may say inappropriate words, or may make incomprehensible sounds. Patients with comas longer than a few days usually have a period of muteness that extends beyond the time when they can again obey simple commands. Therefore, if the coma duration is several days, the patient will begin to speak some time afterward — although occasionally, a patient will say words before obeying simple commands. Patients may have mechanical obstructions that prevent them from speaking when they are neurologically ready, such as a tracheostomy or a wired jaw for a mandibular fracture, or they may have a paralyzed vocal cord.

The patient usually begins to speak during the period of posttraumatic amnesia. Initial language productions indicate the patient's disoriented condition. Speech is usually coherent, but may be dysarthric or dysfluent. Sometimes speech is slow and sometimes it lacks affective prosody, meaning it is devoid of emotional content. When the patient speaks in such a manner, he or she often displays a general lack of emotional reaction. This clinical condition may be difficult to distinguish from depression.

Two language patterns are commonly seen during this period. The first pattern is characterized by sparse language production. The patient is not spontaneous at all, and will answer only when questions are directed to him or her. Then, the patient tends to answer in single words and short phrases. Grammar is usually correct and associations are logical. This pattern is often accompanied by lack of affective prosody.

The second pattern is characterized by excess speech production, that is, verbosity. The patient talks too much, often making a conversational interchange difficult. In addition, associations are tangential, or circumstantial, that is, statements follow from previous statements, but quickly leave the main point of the conversation and drift off into irrelevant material. For example, the patient may make a statement about someone during a conversation but then proceeds to give a complete biography of the person or make inappropriate, irrelevant statements about the person. The associations usually maintain a logical sequence but may become illogical when the patient becomes agitated or overly stressed.

Sometimes during posttraumatic amnesia or when the patient is severely impaired, explanations will be offered for events he or she cannot remember or is confused about. These statements, resulting from erroneous perceptions, are called confabulations and have the quality of made-up stories.

When posttraumatic amnesia terminates and memory function improves, then language functions usually also show improvement. But language impairment sometimes persists as a long-term deficit. If the head injury is open and focal, as from a bullet that traverses a language area in the dominant frontal or temporal lobe, then the patient will often have a residual aphasia, that is, specific deficits in the expressive and receptive components of language. Aphasia is defined and classified in adults by administration of a test battery such as the Aphasia Language Proficiency Scale, The Boston Diagnostic Aphasia Exam, and the Minnesota Test for the Differential Diagnosis of Aphasia (Schwartz, 1989). Tests of specific language function for children include The Boston Naming Test, Rapid Automatized Naming, the Token Test, and tests of phonemic segmentation.

Types of Posttraumatic Language Dysfunction

Both focal and diffuse brain damage characterize closed-head injury. Patients with persistent language deficits after closed-head injury can be divided into two groups (Hagen, 1986). The first group demonstrates specific language deficits with minimal cognitive impairment. Patients in this group will be aphasic when tested. Common language deficits include anomic errors, word finding problems, auditory and reading comprehension deficits, and paraphasic responses. A 2-year study of adult head injury patients in a rehabilitation hospital reported annual incidences of aphasia of 18 and 28% (Stepanik & Roth, 1985).

The second group of patients with persistent language deficits is more common. These patients demonstrate disorganized language secondary to a primary cognitive disorganization. A specific language disorder may coexist with these deficits of language utilization. It is important to distinguish between these two groups, because traditional language therapy for aphasia may be ineffective when cognitive deficits such as memory and attention are primary.

Cognitive functions of concentration, attention, memory, nonverbal problem solving, part/whole analysis and synthesis, conceptual organization, abstract thinking, and speed of processing are intimately related to language formulation and processing. These cognitive functions support language processing and their disruption results in concomitant language disruption. When these cognitive functions are disrupted, it becomes difficult for the patient to have an organized sequential train of thought. As a result, language may appear inappropriate, irrelevant, confabulatory, fragmented, without a logical sequence, tangential, concrete, and confused (Hagen, 1986).

Speech-Language Therapy

The speech-language pathologist helps the patient to maximize residual functions as he or she progresses in cognitive recovery. The Rancho Los Amigos Level of Cognitive Functioning Scale is an instrument that can identify the patient's level of cognitive/communicative functioning throughout the rehabilitation course. (See Appendix C.) This scale has not been adapted successfully for use with children, but is often used with benefit for younger patients.

Speech-language therapy commences within hours of the injury, when the patient is in coma, at levels 1 and 2 on the Rancho Los Amigos Scale. Controlled sensory and sensorimotor stimulation is administered in this early phase with goals of increasing arousal and increasing recognition of people and objects in the environment (Schwartz-Cowley & Stepanik, 1989). The early phase of recovery occurs in the intensive care hospital and during the acute rehabilitation hospitalization.

Patients begin to speak in the middle phase of recovery and the symptoms of cognitive/communicative disorganization may then appear. This middle phase is treated during the rehabilitation hospitalization. It is described by levels 3, 4, and 5 on the Rancho Los Amigos Scale. Treatments aim at minimizing agitation by delivering carefully controlled stimuli that are within the patient's capacity for processing information. Therapeutic procedures include orientation tasks, auditory and visual comprehension tasks, and verbal problem-solving exercises (Schwartz-Cowley & Stepanik, 1989).

The late phase of recovery extends into the postacute rehabilitation period and includes Rancho Los Amigos levels 6 through 8. Sometimes patients attain this phase before discharge from the intensive care hospital, but passage to this phase of recovery sometimes takes months to years. Language and cognitive test results become more reliable during this phase, with increased orientation allowing diagnosis of specific deficits. Patients are assisted in performing cognitive reorganization tasks while a structured environment is maintained. Deficits of attention, memory, comprehension, and executive function are common. Sometimes patients with mild-and-moderate head injury resemble severely head-injured patients who are in the late phase of recovery.

Augmentative Communication Systems

After severe head injury, the ability to communicate may be compromised either temporarily or for a longer period. Communication impairment may be attributed to brain damage or to damage of the peripheral speech mechanism, for example., the larynx. Cognitive and motor impairment may also be present, adding to the severity of the communication impairment and increasing the complexity of its treatment.

Speech-language pathologists help patients to communicate better by providing them with augmentative communication devices. These devices range from homemade communication boards, on which the patient points to letters and pictures, to complex computer systems, equipped with voice and printed outputs. (See Figure 3-3.) Depending on the patient's mobility, these devices may be activated by adapted keyboards, touch monitors, voice activation or switch interfaces (Wilds, 1989).

The speech-language pathologist assesses the optimal physical positions for the patient to communicate, communication partners, locations of communication, and the content of the patient's communicative needs. This team member further assesses the patient's motor, language, and cognitive abilities, as well as the status of his or her vision. In implementing the system, the speech-language pathologist chooses words and phrases to fit the patient's needs (Beukelman, Yorkston, & Dowden, 1985). The specialist trains a facilitator to assume responsibility for ongoing interventions (Light, Beesley, & Collier, 1988). As the patient improves, one communication system may need to be replaced by another. Also, the available technology changes frequently, and there is a wide choice of systems from which individualized communication programs can be constructed (Lahm & Elting, 1989).

FUNCTIONAL OUTCOME MEASURES

As previously stated, studies indicate that functional outcome improves through participation in cognitive rehabilitation programs. Two rating scales are commonly used with adults to sequentially document levels of function after head injury. The Glasgow Outcome Scale has five outcome categories: good

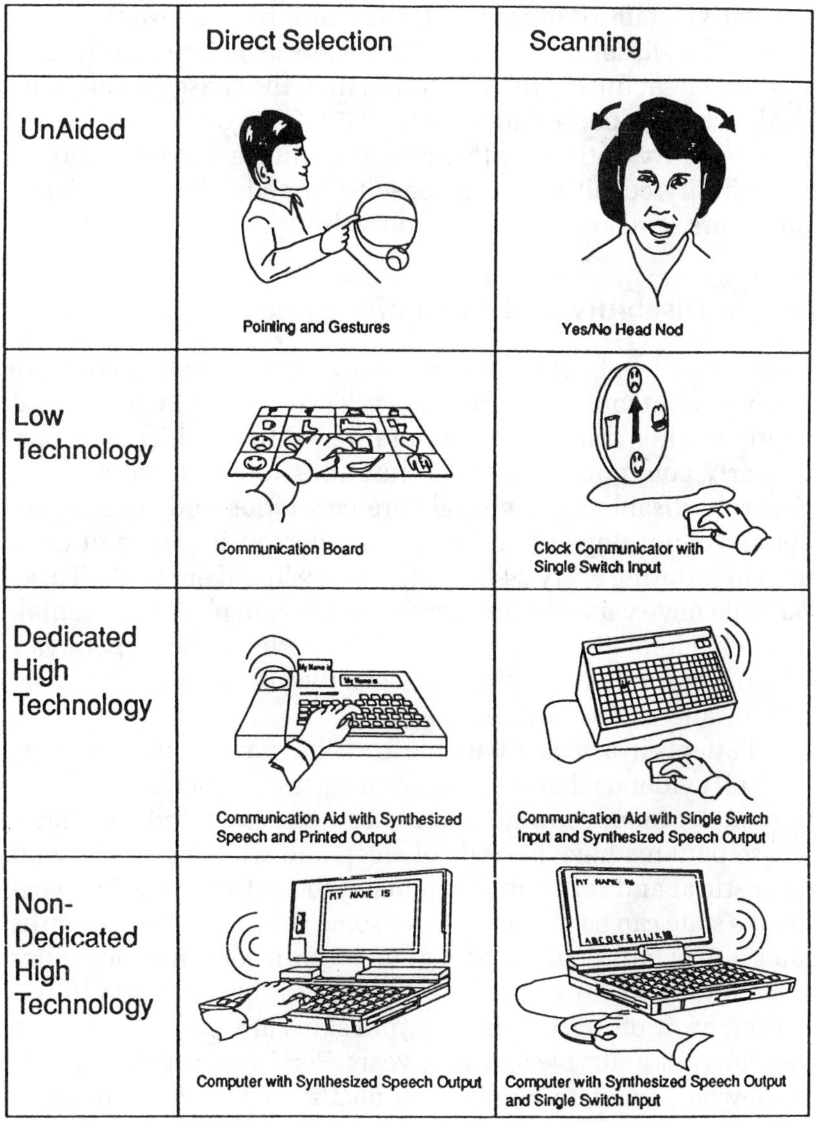

	Direct Selection	Scanning
UnAided	 Pointing and Gestures	 Yes/No Head Nod
Low Technology	 Communication Board	 Clock Communicator with Single Switch Input
Dedicated High Technology	 Communication Aid with Synthesized Speech and Printed Output	 Communication Aid with Single Switch Input and Synthesized Speech Output
Non-Dedicated High Technology	 Computer with Synthesized Speech Output	 Computer with Synthesized Speech Output and Single Switch Input

Figure 3-3. Augmentative communication classification system. Reprinted from Church and Glennen (1992) with permission.

recovery, moderate disability, severe disability, persistent vegetative state, and death (Jennett, Snoek, Bond, & Brooks, 1981). The second scale, the Disability Rating Scale, yields nine disability categories: none, mild, partial, moderate, moderately severe, severe, extremely severe, vegetative state, and extreme vegetative state (Rappaport, Hall, Hopkins, Belleza, & Cope, 1982). The Disability Rating Scale is more sensitive in reflecting improvement during rehabilitation than the Glasgow Outcome Scale (Hall, Cope, & Rappaport, 1985). Categories assessed on the Disability Rating Scale are arousability, awareness and responsibility, cognitive ability for self-care activities, dependence on others, and psychosocial adaptability.

Severe Disability and Vegetative State

Functional levels of severe disability and vegetative state are the worst outcomes of head injury. These conditions are most common after comas of long duration — the incidence is particularly common with coma durations longer than 90 days. Severely disabled individuals are conscious and socially responsive, but dependent on another person for some of their activities during every 24 hours (Jennett & Teasdale, 1981). These patients have varying combinations of severe physical, mental, and behavioral disabilities. Disabilities include spastic paralysis of three or four extremities, aphasia, dysarthria, impaired cognition, and disinhibition.

Patients in a vegetative state are behaviorally unresponsive, with no evidence that their cerebral cortex is functioning. They may make inappropriate sounds or even say words at times. These patients have periods of sleep and wakefulness as well as postural and reflex movements of the extremities. The vegetative state can be predicted with some confidence by 3 months after injury, although some patients regain consciousness after more than 100 days of coma. With fastidious attention to nutrition, positioning, respiratory, and skin care, patients who are vegetative can survive for many years. Persistent vegetative state is viewed as a state worse than death because the patient is unresponsive and the family must continue to care for a living person who cannot communicate with them.

PSYCHIATRIC IMPAIRMENT, BEHAVIORAL AND EMOTIONAL

Psychiatric problems, behavioral and emotional, are very common after head injury and their presence contributes significantly to a poor late outcome. Brown describes a high rate of behavioral and emotional impairment after severe closed-head injury in children who did not have premorbid impairment. In her prospective study, more than 50% of head-injured children without antecedent psychiatric problems developed these problems in the 2 1/4 years after their injury (Brown, Chadwick, Shaffer, Rutter, & Traub, 1981). It is those children and adolescents with behavioral or cognitive impairment or both who are most likely to be discharged to inpatient rehabilitation hospitals (Di Scala et al., 1991).

Psychiatric problems are prominent during acute rehabilitation hospitalization and often persist into the postacute phase of community reentry. These problems of early recovery abate and may be replaced at any time, even months or years later, by new behavioral or emotional problems. In fact, adult postacute rehabilitation programs tend to admit unstable disabled persons who are functioning poorly and most adults in these postacute programs are treated for behavioral and emotional problems (Johnston & Lewis, 1991). These problems may continue, or new psychiatric problems may appear after discharge from the postacute program.

The late outcome study of Inger Thomsen (1984) after severe closed-head injury documents changes in personality and emotions in two-thirds of adult patients 10 to 15 years after injury. These changes were more frequent among patients who had been injured before the age of 21. The main impairments were rapid changes between apathy and aggression, irritability, and childishness, with resultant development of poor family relationships. In this long-term follow-up study, 20% of the 40 patients developed posttraumatic psychoses, with onset from 3 months to 9 years after the injury.

Posttraumatic psychiatric impairment is classified according to the time of occurrence. Early posttraumatic problems occur before termination of the posttraumatic amnesia, and the symptoms collectively are called delirium. Manifestations of delirium described in Chapter 2 are neurologically determined, although probably modified by pretraumatic personality traits. The onset of late posttraumatic psychiatric problems occurs first at the termination of the posttraumatic amnesia when the patient is alert, oriented, and again in possession of his or her senses. It is this late collection of behaviors and emotional states that adversely affects the long-term functional adjustment of the patient. Improvement in the diagnosis and treatment of these psychiatric problems will lead to a more successful community reentry and to an improved long-term outcome.

The likelihood of developing psychiatric problems after closed-head injury is related to the severity of injury, the location of injury, the child's premorbid behavioral/emotional status, and to his or her psychosocial circumstances. Also, children with psychiatric disorder are at increased risk for the occurrence of head injury. The more severe the injury, the more likely the development of psychiatric impairment. Injury to specific brain locations, for example, the frontal lobe, is more likely to result in psychiatric impairment. Children with premorbid psychiatric symptoms are much more likely to demonstrate posttraumatic psychiatric problems than children who do not have these problems. And children who are members of dysfunctional families are at increased risk for the development of post-traumatic psychiatric disorders.

Late Posttraumatic Psychiatric Impairment

The behavioral and emotional disorders occurring after termination of posttraumatic amnesia are the same disorders that can occur in children and adolescents who have not had head injury. If symptoms of inattention, depression, or anxiety were present before the injury, then these symptoms will remain the same or intensify after the posttraumatic amnesia terminates. Symptoms of inattention, hyperactivity, and easy distractibility are commonly described in the premorbid histories of children who have suffered closed-head injury.

Frontal Lobe Psychiatric Impairment

The frontal and temporal lobes are frequently damaged during closed-head injury. Psychiatric symptoms in adults are seen more frequently after focal frontal lobe damage in an open-head injury than after damage to other cerebral areas, and include aggression, disinhibition, demandingness, childishness, and euphoria. Apathy, slowness of movement, and decreased speech production are also attributed to focal frontal lobe damage. Children demonstrate similar disinhibited patterns of behavior after severe closed-head injury that involves the frontal lobes, with symptoms being overtalkativeness, disregard for social convention, carelessness in personal hygiene and dress, and impulsivity (Rutter, 1981).

Temporal Lobe Psychiatric Impairment

The temporal lobes are also particularly susceptible to damage in closed-head injury (Mattson & Levin, 1990). Psychiatric symptoms seen in patients with focal temporal lobe damage after open-head injury include suspiciousness or paranoid ideation, exaggerated aggressiveness, humorless overtalkativeness, and preoccupation with religious subjects (Herrington, 1969). Focal temporal damage, particularly on the left side of the brain, is associated with increased risk for the development of a psychosis similar to schizophrenia (Hillbom, 1960). However a definite group of psychiatric symptoms attributed to temporal lobe closed-head injury has not yet been described.

Psychiatric Impairment After Mild-and-Moderate Head Injury

The constellation of neurologic, neuropsychologic, emotional, and behavioral symptoms that occur after mild head injury in adults is called the postconcussion syndrome. These symptoms include headache, dizziness, memory loss, emotional lability, increased sensitivity to sound, impaired concentration, disinhibition, depression, lost work, and fatigue and last for several weeks to a year after injury (Rimel, Giordani, Barth, Boll, & Jane, 1981; Stevens, 1984). These are the same symptoms that occur after severe injuries, but are generally less severe and are usually unaccompanied by motor problems. Headache is seen frequently after mild head injury, but only occasionally after severe head injury. Many of these symptoms, for example, dizziness, vertigo, insomnia, cranial nerve abnormalities, appear to be the result of brainstem dysfunction. The postconcussion syndrome clinical picture for children is probably similar to that of adults, with additional symptoms of worsened behaviors. Sometimes, the only impairment after a mild closed-head injury to a child or adult will be development of severe psychiatric problems. The postconcussion syndrome must be taken into consideration after mild injuries, as the patient will suffer much if his or her distress is ignored and if expected to resume a previous high level of functioning. Moderate head injury, defined as an admission Glasgow Coma Scale score of 9 to 12, often results in considerable neuropsychological impairment, but the nature, extent, and duration of psychiatric impairment have not been defined for this group (Knights et al., 1991).

Relationship to delinquent and criminal behavior

The relationship between head injury and subsequent delinquent behavior is an important one. Lewis, Shanok, and Balla (1979) reported that incarcerated delinquents were significantly more likely to have previously sustained a head or facial injury (62.3%) than nonincarcerated delinquents (44.6%). Child abuse was noted more frequently in the medical charts of incarcerated children (10.4%) than in the charts of nonincarcerated children (3.6%). Other studies of delinquents have documented a higher incidence of head injuries with longer coma durations within the study populations. Neuropsychologic assessment of delinquent youths has revealed wide-spread abnormalities in cognitive, memory, speech, perceptual and perceptual motor areas. Learning disabilities are also common (Robbins, Beck, Pries, Jacobs, & Smith, 1983).

Severe head injury, often multiple, is frequently present in the histories of juveniles and adults imprisoned for homicide. The majority of these prisoners have neurologic, psychiatric, and neuropsychologic impairments demonstrated by formal testing. In one study of 15 death-row inmates, all of the inmates had histories of severe head injury and 12 had neurologic impairment. Six inmates were chronically psychotic and two others were manic-depressive (Lewis, Pincus, Feldman, Jackson, & Bard, 1986).

Treatment of Behavioral and Emotional Impairment

Treatment of posttraumatic psychiatric impairment is interdisciplinary and involves all of the treating disciplines. Maladaptive behavioral and emotional states affect all aspects of rehabilitation. Therefore, all the therapists need to participate in the treatment program to achieve a beneficial outcome.

Treatment may begin in the acute rehabilitation hospital or in a community reentry program.

A behavior modification system provides the framework for many neurobehavioral programs. Such a program may be organized as a token economy and may also include patient and family counseling, social skills training, therapeutic recreation, and treatment of substance abuse. The primary goal of programs that treat posttraumatic psychiatric disorders is to replace maladaptive behaviors with positive behaviors that generalize to everyday life and to eliminate pathologic emotional states.

Although all rehabilitation disciplines participate in behavioral/emotional treatment, the basic treatment team consists of a psychiatrist, a behavioral psychologist, a social worker, and a therapeutic recreation specialist. The psychiatrist diagnoses the patient's disorder, provides psychotherapy, and prescribes medication when it is necessary to treat severe disorders that can include anxiety, depression, psychosis, and disruptive behavior. The behavioral psychologist constructs and administers a behavioral reinforcement program that is adapted for use in the home, school, and community. The social worker assesses the family's ability to provide for and support its head-injured member. Family members are counseled and helped to negotiate the complicated health care system. As the productive use of leisure is important to the emotional stability of disabled persons' lives, the specialist in therapeutic recreation assists the patient in the choice of suitable and worthwhile activities (Johnston & Lewis, 1991).

SUMMARY

The rehabilitation of head-injured children and adolescents is a lengthy process that may extend into months and years. Acute rehabilitation takes place in hospitals, and includes treatment of persistent medical problems, as well as assessment and treatment of physical, cognitive, and psychiatric impairments. Postacute rehabilitation care is given in the special education setting, where comprehensive rehabilitation services include occupational therapy, physical therapy, speech-language therapy, and counseling. Neuropsychologic and behavioral impairments receive special emphasis in the educational plan, as these impairments occur frequently and their persistence contributes significantly to a poor late outcome.

Chapter 4

Implications for School Planning

VARIABILITY

The first lesson a therapist or teacher learns about children and adolescents who have sustained closed-head injury is that they are each unique, and thus their cognitive, psychomotor, and psychosocial profiles are unpredictable. These elusive profiles can change quite rapidly, especially during early recovery. In fact, the one attribute common to children and adolescents who have sustained closed head injury is *variability* . Nowhere is variability the cause for more difficulty than in school planning.

Variability permeates all dimensions of recovery. While it is possible to generalize about this population and attempt to predict patterns of recovery, the fact that each youngster will digress from the general pattern must not be overlooked.

Prognosis

Typically, a child's rate of change during the first 6 months following the injury is dramatic. Measurable differences can be found from one day to the next, and sometimes from morning to evening. The rapid change tapers off in the ensuing months but some degree of change can continue for years. Even in the early period, recovery can be discouragingly slow for some patients. For the unfortunate, there is little change from one week to the next.

Such factors as length of coma and length of PTA, previously discussed, serve as long-term prognostic indicators, but do little for planning the therapeutic interventions to be used during those first months following closed-head injury.

Impairment

As has been previously described, not all head injuries result in the same nature or degree of impairment. The variability of effects from the injury will be influenced by the particular areas of the brain in which the injury occurred (e.g., frontal lobe, brainstem, parietal lobe, and so forth) and the extent of the deficits (e.g., mild, moderate, or severe; cognitive, psychomotor, or psychosocial).

Injury sites do not recover at the same rate. Thus, while speech may be restored within a few days, integrated thinking processes may take months or years. In fact "recovery" does not necessarily imply a full restoration to preinjury status. It is a relative term, and more realistically represents the reacquisition of a percentage of those abilities a person once had. Thus, the extent of damage, the location of injury, and the recovery process, itself, are variable in each individual.

Memory Processes

Head-injured patients consistently suffer amnesia of events surrounding and immediately following their injury. Even when a patient has passed the termination of posttraumatic amnesia, memory processes are usually erratic. In the reacquisition of academics, a youngster will sometimes regain a very specific skill, such as spelling, while experiencing severe deficits across the cognitive domain. As recovery progresses, the patient's recall of previously learned material continues. Generally, quantitative concepts (e.g., application of numerical operations, measurement) are recalled sooner than number facts and processes used in calculation. Reading recognition improves to within normal limits long before comprehension of reading passages. Visual problem solving and mathematics skills may remain intact in a child or adolescent who demonstrates severe aphasia. Thus, some predictability exists within the variable recovery process.

Preinjury Achievement

In addition to the variability in injury and recovery rate, each patient's individuality must be taken into account. Academic achievement following closed-head injury is affected by premorbid learning preferences and rates of achievement. The youngster's preinjury achievement has an obvious direct effect on what is available for recall. Any preexisting learning problems will remain; actually, they more often are exacerbated by the injury.

Treatment Differences

Variability among patients includes differences in the treatment received from the time of emergency care to school readmission. (See Figure 4-1.) Some patients will be transferred from an

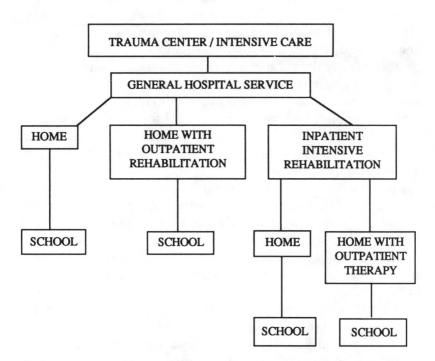

Figure 4-1. Various scenarios of treatment following pediatric head injury

intensive care unit to a general hospital service and then discharged home when medical status is stable. They may, in some cases, experience no difficulty in returning to former activities, including school. Others who have been discharged directly to home, will exhibit such disruptive and provocative behaviors as agitation, severe amnesia, and disorientation–especially in the early stages of recovery — which must then be played out within the care of the family. During this stage, loss of immediate memory can be so severe that returning a youngster to school would have no purpose other than a custodial one. A patient at this stage, for example, might ask repeatedly for accounts of the accident. The patient's need to learn and remember what has happened is prominent, but the vehicle for recalling is insufficient for even this fundamental piece of information.

Still other patients are discharged from intensive care units to tertiary settings such as rehabilitation programs where medical and therapeutic needs, both physical and cognitive, are addressed. Admission to such a facility presumes that this resource is available within a reasonable distance for at least weekly visits by families, and that it is accessible (i.e., there must be empty beds). Families must be able to meet heavy financial burdens for medical bills through insurance or other means. For many patients, this type of treatment is not an option.

Rightfully the subject of current research, the process and value of cognitive rehabilitation is not detailed here. For more information on this topic, see Levin (1990) , Berrol (1990) and Volpe, Fletcher, and McDowell (1990) for their reviews.

Patients with the option of rehabilitation, however, are at considerable advantage in their readiness to return to school. For example, the course of recovery and its quality can be influenced by stimulation, intensive therapy, structure, and careful management during the critical period of rapid posttraumatic change. In theory, a patient who is surrounded by a staff that consistently responds to agitated, confused, and disorganized behavior, may be at less risk of developing maladaptive patterns of physical, cognitive, and psychosocial behavior that can be carried into school. Generally, families and educators cannot be expected to have the personal resources, knowledge, or objectivity for optimal care of children during this stage of recovery. Even when families can intellectually accept that their children might not be responsible for behavior during the immediate postcoma period, they often find a child's behavior painfully embarrassing. It is much easier for a professional staff member to interpret any lack of control as disinhibition created by injury, and then matter-of-factly ignore the behavior or instruct the patient that the behavior was inappropriate — confident that as the brain heals, the disinhibition will abate. The same confidence and objectivity are needed by teachers if they face undesirable or inappropriate behaviors when the patient returns to school.

Thus, school planning is made tentative not only by the differences in the rate and progress of recovery of each individual, but also by the variability in the degree and nature of impairment, in preinjury achievement and intelligence, and in the course of the treatment itself.

COMMON NEEDS

Structure

There are several needs common to all head-injured students. In the hospital setting, structure is inherent in the routine administration of care, medication, therapies, meals, and visiting hours. In a rehabilitation hospital this structure is increased in a regimen which includes more therapies. Many patients will have physical, occupational, speech, and cognitive/academic therapies several times daily; they also will likely participate in orientation groups and recreational activities. Schedules are adhered to closely and only abandoned for medical tests or intervention. Such a tightly scheduled day frees these children and adolescents from initiating activities or making decisions.

Patients with recent injuries do not organize themselves into constructive activities. Initiation, motivation, and judgment are absent. Thus, for the weeks immediately following injury and for many weeks beyond, caregivers must provide structure as a vehicle for carrying out daily living activities. This is equally true for school activity. Return to school, with inherent class and activity schedules provides a much needed structure within which the youngster can function. However, activity must continually be more narrowly defined with each class in the schedule, each activity in the class, and each assignment in the activity reinforcing and developing structure. For example, no returning student who has sustained head injury is likely to benefit from assignment to a study hall or library where independent work is expected. A teacher must tightly organize the class schedule to provide supervision and assistance during every period in the school day. If a student might benefit from a period allowing additional time to complete assignments, this period must be supervised and structured for success.

Within instructional periods, a teacher's written and oral directions need to be specific and task oriented, providing clear expectations for the student. For example, a teacher can expect poor results from an assignment asking a student to write a composition about the class field trip to an aquarium. Added structure is needed, such as, "Write about two major differences between the seals and the sharks you observed in the aquarium. You may focus on their natural habitats, their habits, or their characteristics. The composition should be about two pages and at least three paragraphs. It is due the day after tomorrow." To the student who has sustained a head injury the teacher might also say "I would like to see your outline tomorrow." Teachers should not fear they are depriving students with head injuries by restricting their choices. These students function best when provided with organization, clearly stated expectations, systematic and consistent routine, and limited choices. Provided with only a basic schedule of classes, the student may not be able to proceed independently. It is the teacher's continuing provision of structure, down to details of the assignment in front of the student, that clarifies and helps enable what is required. Rather than stifling the head-injured student, the teacher is enhancing the youngster's chance for success.

Structure, then, is perhaps the most important invariable need of the student who has sustained head injury. A discussion of methods to develop structure and to modify this environment as the recovering youngster's needs change is provided in Chapter 7.

Flexibility

When returning to school following a head injury, students are doubly penalized. During their absence, they have missed whole units of instruction, and moreover, they are likely returning with reduced abilities to function at even an average rate, much less also make up the lessons missed. Although hospital tutoring is generally available, its effectiveness is reduced for the following reasons:

- By the time patients have enough memory to begin studying again, it is often almost time to be discharged.
- Tutoring competes with medical and therapeutic attention and has less priority in a medical setting.
- Tutoring may prepare students, somewhat, for the difficulties they face in learning; but, otherwise, it is often too little to compensate for the losses.

Thus, the school staff needs to be flexible in their requirements regarding Carnegie units and credits when considering placement at the time of a student's return. Students return to school at a great disadvantage, requiring accommodation and time: time to make up what has been missed; extended time for tests and assignment completion; time taken by teachers for repeating directions and giving extra assistance; time to get from one place in the building to another — in essence, time to recover. Flexibility is required to strike the best balance between requirements and necessary accommodations.

Reduced Demands

In hand with flexibility is the need to reduce demands made on students who have sustained head injuries. At the secondary level, this may include substitution of less demanding classes for the subjects studied premorbidly or of substitution of totally new subjects for those which require heavy reading or written assignments, abstraction, much memorization, or complex language. The student's reading comprehension and speed are likely to be well below grade level. For elementary and secondary students, alike, extension of time limits reduces the amount of required work into more achievable units and is integral to success during this reintegration period.

Although there are times when the teacher's objective is aimed at developing decoding and reading comprehension, there are also times when information acquisition is the goal. At these times, any method helping the student receive the information is acceptable. Thus, parents may be encouraged to read information to their children or to use audiotapes. Students faced with reading novels for English assignments might use audiotapes to enhance comprehension. Such tapes are available from state resources for the blind (also available to students with learning disabilities), public libraries, and through commercial companies such as Books on Tape (1-800-626-3333).

Parents and teachers should be cautioned that sometimes their child's listening comprehension might also be poor because of difficulties with attention, memory, or auditory processing. In these cases, the value of using taped material is reduced.

Traditional timed, written tests might be too demanding for head-injured students. This may dictate the need to administer oral tests (perhaps by the resource teacher) and to extend time limits. Perhaps a student can be assigned a project to demonstrate a skill or concept attainment in lieu of a lengthy written assignment. In general, teachers should construct tests and assignments to measure recognition rather than recall. If given at all, memorization assignments will be more successful if their content is organized for ease of learning and recall. Mnemonic cues for self-prompting may need to be employed. Although the need for memory in everyday life cannot be ignored, teachers should avoid the use of rote memory tasks as a measure of learning achievement.

Modifying expectations of independence may also be necessary. Teachers and parents should no longer assume that a secondary school head-injured student can be entirely independent and responsible for his or her work. A student who has sustained head injury may forget to turn in completed homework, lose assignments, or fail to write them down in the first place. The student's impaired language comprehension may so reduce independent functioning that instructions will need to be consistently rephrased or repeated.

The value of notetaking is lost to most head-injured students because the task itself is so overwhelming that its purpose is secondary. A student's efficiency may be severely reduced by a combination of poor listening comprehension; hemiplegia, or weakness in the dominant hand; inability to recognize the most salient information, and distraction. Borrowing notes from a successful student, or using notes written on special duplicating (carbon) paper by a peer provides students with information that they cannot acquire independently. This can be vital for tutors and parents trying to help head-injured students prepare assignments or study new material.

Supervision

What supervision do students who have sustained head injury require in the school setting? In elementary schools, where physical space and class size are generally on a smaller scale, not much more than ordinary supervision may be required. At the secondary level, the size of physical plant, the number of students in the building, and the frequency of social contact among students make supervision more difficult.

For a poorly oriented student, trips to the lavatory, for example, can be a source of trouble depending on others who might be in the rest room. One patient initiated conversation with others using the facilities and, totally distracted by the interchange, ended up following them back to their classes, becoming lost.

The poor judgment and naiveté common among students who have sustained head injuries leave them especially susceptible to persuasion and vulnerable to adolescent humor, teasing, and practical jokes. Cafeterias and corridors are minefields for these students. These areas are the bane of supervision for most staff. Sometimes "buddies" can be enlisted to carry books and trays, orient to place, and befriend in the cafeteria. Sometimes, however, befriending a student who has sustained head injury means jeopardizing one's own social standing, especially if the injured student's behavior is conspicuous or misunderstood.

With a built-in capability for monitoring and supervising a wide range of student activities, the guidance staff can be used as intermediaries among students, and between students and teachers; guidance counselors can provide coordination and communication among the various people involved with the student. This service is especially useful in secondary schools. The guidance office is often preferable to a study hall, and a student assigned there once a day can be given simple tasks while a counselor monitors him or her for changes. This also establishes a contact between the head-injured student and one key person when general assistance is needed.

A student's more subtle needs for supervision fall in the realm of teacher planning, whether in organizing daily work or planning long-range assignments. Some degree of supervision may need to be built into the design of the assignment.

Intervention

Deficits as the result of head injury are usually physically unseen. Thus, students who have been victims of head injury are not always conspicuous, nor are they always known to their teachers. Early identification of these students' needs provides potential stress prevention, both for the youngster and the school staff. Nearly all youngsters who have sustained head injury will require some intervention. Without such intervention, staff and student risk increased failure, misunderstanding, inappropriate demands, and seeming indifference.

TRANSITIONS FROM HOSPITAL TO HOME

Timing

When a patient is discharged from a therapeutic rehabilitative setting, they have generally recovered memory functions and control of behavior sufficiently to be amenable to participation in school, if only in a limited way. Thus, when this text suggests that immediate return to school is encouraged, it is in reference to patients who have recovered to this extent.

The urgency of early school return is often questioned by parents and school staff. As variability and the dynamic characteristics of recovery can make school planning more difficult, it might be asked if return to school should be delayed until the patient's changing mental status stabilizes.

There are several justifications for an early return to school. Patients face an approaching date of discharge with ambivalence about leaving the hospital. On the one hand, a return home marks a major step in recovery. On the other hand, they may have been in the hospital long enough to have become comfortable with the security of a place where their needs have been anticipated and met. Eager as a patient may be to leave, the world beyond may seem quite frightening. Their eagerness is mixed with dread. Ideally, the patient will have spent a few trial weekends at home practicing therapy goals. To stay at home for good becomes a goal in itself. For some, home is viewed as a haven; it can be an escape to one's room, without demands, or outsiders — so comfortable that it may be hard to leave.

If a patient leaves the hospital with an expectation of return to "normal" life, then returning to school is a part of this self-perception of normalcy. Returning home includes returning to school if one is to fit in with peers. To be at home, but not to return to school emphasizes a youngster's disability and invites a prolonged perception as an invalid. Under these circumstances, it is unlikely that the patient will find return to school any easier at some future date.

Although early return is encouraged, all involved must realize that it is as shaky a step psychologically as it is physically. Children will have lost the comfortable familiarity of friends because of their prolonged absence. They may have scars or other evidence of injury that set them apart. As hospital patients,they were generally aware of being different from the persons they once were, but they were not fundamentally different from those around them in that setting. This "fitting in" affords a certain amount of comfort and consolation. Patients can even appreciate when another patient's condition is worse than theirs by comparison. To return to school, however, is to return alone and different — different from the person they once were and different from their peers.

Available Services

Before their injury, most of these children followed a typical growth and achievement developmental course. Even in cases where children have previously encountered problems, parents considered them average. More to the point, most of these children were not handicapped at birth. This factor contributes to their uniqueness, as the normal course of development has now been disrupted. Parents find themselves in the position of accepting a new child. They have to develop new expectations of what their son or daughter can or cannot do. Because the handicap is recent and parents have had little experience with it, they often inaccurately predict what is possible.

School staff are equally as inexperienced in teaching students who have sustained severe head trauma, largely because the condition has been rare in school populations. Medical advances, particularly in trauma care, have increased the number of survivors of such injuries; but in relation to the whole student population, they represent only a small percentage. Thus, both parents and educational staff are at risk for holding unrealistic or uncertain expectations.

In light of this discussion, a patient's immediate return to school at the end of hospitalization is often discounted as a possibility. If unfamiliar with services available for students with disabilities, a parent may worry about transportation for their child who is still using a wheelchair for mobility. They may worry about whether the school can provide the degree of supervision their child now requires. Parents of average children who have suddenly become parents of a child with a handicap will need to learn much about what is provided in the school system.

Public Law 94-142 and its subsequent amendments provide for education of children and adolescents who have sustained head injury. A mandate for public education for all students who are handicapped, the law outlines the structure through which these students may be assessed for eligibility, defines the nature of the handicap, details the ancillary therapeutic services to which children are entitled, and provides a time frame within which they must be provided. Access to these benefits is further defined by each state in its interpretation of the federal mandate.

Public Law 101-476, which amends Public Law 94-142, is called the Individuals with Disabilities Education Act, and now defines traumatic head injury as a handicapping condition under the category "Other health impaired." In itself, this is helpful as it frees schools from having to use other less accurate handicapping conditions for qualifying these youngsters for services under the law. Even so, the nature of traumatic head injury, with its sudden onset and dynamic characteristics, presents some problems in accessing services under the law.

For example, the time constraints and qualifying evaluations that are designed to protect students from inappropriate labeling and placement, sometimes work to the disadvantage of children with head injuries. Schools need lead time to plan to gather medical reports, assess, organize staff for review and assignment, schedule transportation, and provide therapies. By law, interdisciplinary meetings must be held in order to review assessment findings and to develop an individual education plan for each aspect of student activity. On the other hand, the nature and course of recovery is unpredictable enough to impede advance planning. Planning needs will change within 2 weeks of recovery for some children. Yet those changes cannot be predicted dependably, and educational plans cannot be developed on the basis of what might be needed. Occasionally, patients become ready for discharge quickly, allowing insufficient time for school readmission, especially if special education services are needed. Inadequate preparation for a student's school reentry leads to loss of valuable time and delays an optimal transition from hospital to home and/or school.

An important special education provision of Public Law 94-142 is that children must be assigned to the least restrictive school environment needed to accomplish learning. The range of services begins with such minimal intervention as specialist consultation with the classroom teacher regarding the needs of a given student. The intensity of intervention increases to include periods of placement in a special class and extends to full-time placement within a residential school. Philosophically, the law reflects the right and need for a child to learn in the most normal setting possible. It may be that a student's deficits are severe enough to warrant a full-time placement in a self-contained classroom, or even in a special wing or unit apart from the main stream. If so, the law provides such; if not, the law safeguards against undue isolation and limitation of movement within regular schools.

It is often the policy of a school system to initially provide the setting that appears to be the least restrictive and to then increase the intensity of services if a youngster demonstrates a lack of progress. For the child who has sustained head trauma, this is not the best tactic. In general, it is preferable to provide increased structure and intervention at initial reentry and gradually reduce the intensity of services as the needs of the student dictate.

As previously stated, this population represents a growing, but small percentage of students receiving special education services. There are only a few programs in the United States designed to meet the unique needs of the traumatically head injured. Such programs are best offered in a regional model rather than for individual school jurisdictions. Model programs will be described in Chapter 5. When such a program is not available, the optimal placement choice within an existing program is not always clear.

The extent of cognitive and behavioral impairment of head-injured youth, along with the long-range need for therapies, impinge on and complicate placement decisions. Cognitive profiles of youngsters who have sustained head injury are not always compatible with those of students who have learning disabilities. Children and adolescents who have sustained head injury, while demonstrating very specific and intrusive processing disorders, often regain previous learning; whereas a youngster who is learning disabled may never have acquired comparable academic mastery. Children who present with poor outcome from head trauma are not always analogous to the mentally retarded for the same reasons. Youngsters with a poor motor outcome are often recommended for placement in a comprehensive special education center where therapists are readily available on a daily basis. In such settings they may not have appropriate cognitive peers. Children who receive psychiatric services under Public Law 94-142 are labeled emotionally disturbed or emotionally handicapped. The socially inappropriate, out-of-control behaviors of some children who have sustained head trauma resemble those of certain emotionally disturbed students. Indeed, some head injury does result in long-term psychiatric disturbance. For the most part, however, poor judgment and loss of control are temporary effects of head injury. In summary, the demand for short-range, intensive services is not always easily accommodated by a system whose primary purpose is education.

In concert with the continuum of special education services other options can be considered.

Home Instruction

In Maryland, a minimum of 4 weeks of need is required to schedule home instruction, because of the startup administrative cost and effort required to arrange for home tutors. Typically,

6 hours of home instruction are scheduled weekly. Home teaching is not to be confused with enrichment teaching or remedial tutoring, but is usually utilized as a substitute to school instruction rather than a supplement. Students are generally not given home instruction in addition to school instruction, but with more awareness of the needs of youngsters who have sustained head injury some school districts are making exceptions.

Combination of Home and School Program

When home instruction is combined with school visits, the school visits may be for socialization only. One student, for example, visited the school at lunch time each day and was included in a brief homeroom activity that followed lunch. Occupational therapy was given before her return to home teaching later in the afternoon. Somewhere in the schedule, the student took a nap. Newly discharged patients often fatigue easily and need rest interspersed during the day, even when they are beyond the typical age for napping.

Reduced School Program

Some youngsters have enough stamina for a full day's physical activity, but they need a lowered dose of activities that require concentration. A patient's gradual return to school can be coordinated with his or her gradual return of function. With this option, resumption of a full-day schedule may be preceded by a partial-day schedule for the first few weeks. The reduced day may include time with a resource teacher or study in a less-demanding class. This decision should be based on the degree and rate of the student's cognitive return. The extent of his or her motor handicap may also play a part. Logistical issues such as the fit of the class within the student's day or the location of the classroom should also be considered in the plan.

Modified School Program

A modified school program differs from a reduced program in that the student attends for the entire day. Within a full-day schedule less demanding classes are substituted for classes in the student's previous schedule, and other creative options are considered. In one instance, parents paid for a private tutor to work with their son during the school day. The student, a senior who had not fulfilled the junior English requirement, worked with the tutor on this goal during one class period, while studying with the senior English class in another. In other instances, teachers have volunteered their planning periods to tutor students in make-up work. Noninstructional personnel such as media specialists, administrators, and guidance counselors can provide options for creative programming. These are examples of the extent to which a school will go to reintegrate a former student, particularly when he or she was a well-liked student or one with academic or vocational promise.

Special Education Programs

In keeping with the law's mandate to provide education in the least restrictive environment, it is preferable to place students in their home schools and supply help from resource teachers for remaining areas of difficulty. Some students can maintain academic levels with this amount of support. Others have pervasive deficits to warrant placement in a self-contained classroom for all subjects. Occasionally, students in such a program are able to join a regular classroom for lunch, gym, or art. Students with more complicated learning problems are assisted by special education teachers in special wings or schools. This physical isolation from the standard classroom is an acknowledgement that their problems of learning and behavior are too severe to be managed in a regular class for even a short time. Except for a residential school, this is the most restrictive setting. (See Figure 4-2.)

No Services; Return to Same Class

It is important to remember that not all students with head injuries have severe deficits. Some can return to school successfully without further intervention. Of this group, some need services, but are not identified and provided with them. Even if the student's deficits are not severe enough to warrant special education, the school staff should realize that even mild difficulties will be intrusive for the student; some minor adaptations within the regular program may suffice. Other students with relatively good outcomes following injury have met more severe problems after return to school. For example, one student

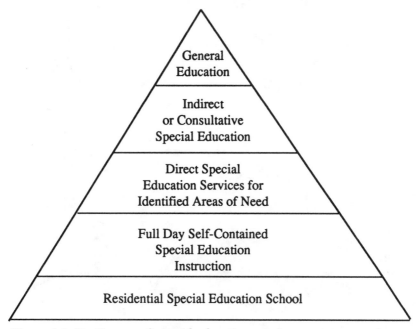

Figure 4-2. Continuum of special education services.

a half year of school. Summer school had not been an option because of his hospital discharge timing. He was an intelligent but uneven-achieving student. In the school's judgment it was best that he review and learn by repeating the ninth grade, but it was the last place the student wanted to be. He began to hate school, most of his teachers, and some of his peers. These problems could have been predicted, but other solutions escaped those planning his return. His first few months back in school erupted into a no-win situation until escalating behavior warranted special education intervention. He was placed in a special school for students with psychiatric problems. It is not known if such psychiatric problems would have emerged if the student had been provided a well-designed, individualized program.

These program options are among the most frequently employed in reintegrating a student who has experienced head injury. When planning the reentry, parents and school staff should start with a blank slate and fill the needs as identified, rather than try to find a close fit for a youngster in existing programs. Creativity and flexibility are the themes for success. Further discussion of the steps in planning for school reentry and suggested strategies for a smooth transition follow in Chapter 5.

Chapter 5

Reintegration: The Process

Rehabilitation professionals working with children who have sustained traumatic head injury will find much of the current literature focuses on adult survivors. After all, the largest age group that experiences traumatic head injury consists of teens and young adults. In some respects, the characteristics of adults and children are similar, as all tend to experience many of the same cognitive and motoric sequelae as they progress through recovery. In designing programs for children, however, normal growth and development enters as a variable. Thus, Savage and Carter (1988) feel that, "the dynamics of school reentry and long-term success are sometimes more complex than returning to work or being trained in a new vocational area."

Scales such as the Ranchos Los Amigos Levels of Cognitive Functioning (Malkmus, Booth, & Kodimer, 1980) assist families and clinicians in predicting the behavioral manifestations of recovery from coma. There are some accepted prognostic indicators of degree of recovery expected (i.e., length of coma and length of PTA), but none that dependably predict the pace of recovery. Normal growth and development, the dynamic recovery process, and the variable rate at which it proceeds, require that the school reintegration process be handled carefully.

COMMON PROBLEMS

Interagency Relations

By their nature, the medical and the educational models differ fundamentally. Many physicians make independent diagnoses, in light of specific symptoms or medical findings, which are treated as prescribed. In contrast, in the special education model, the "whole child" must be considered by a variety of professionals and family members before adaptations to the youngster's regimen are suggested. Sometimes the meshing of these two systems causes friction rather than smooth reentry for the student facing return to school following head trauma.

Rehabilitation programs more closely resemble the educational model and, when a youngster has the benefit of rehabilitation following injury, the chances of a smooth transition are probably better than those returning directly from an acute medical setting. In either case, a reciprocal commitment to interagency coordination is necessary for effective school reentry.

Commonly, a pediatrician, familiar with the laws governing the provision of special education services, might inform a family that therapy and cognitive reeducation will be provided by the school system. However, the physician may be unaware of specific parameters for provision of therapy within an educational context. Thus, what the parents are led to expect can differ considerably from what can be provided.

In some instances, the physician is not sensitive to the cognitive and psychosocial effects of head injury. When a patient is pronounced medically stable and displays no physical needs, he or she may be discharged and cleared to return to school without considering the cognitive and psychosocial problems that can arise. Schools may then be faced with a student who experiences failure because a lack of information did not allow for more careful planning.

For the head-injured child or adolescent, interagency cooperation and mutual orientation to the respective models of operation, are paramount to the smooth transition from hospital to school and community.

Availability of Programs or Staff

Within the educational system, as it currently operates, a child returning to school following traumatic head injury has the option of returning to a general education program or seeking an Individualized Educational Program (IEP) through the provisions of Public Law 94-142, the Education of the Handicapped Act (EHA), and Public Law 101-476, the new Individuals with Disabilities Education Act (IDEA) that amended P.L. 94-142 in 1990. For most students who have experienced any significant degree of difficulty following traumatic head injury, it is advisable to seek special education services.

By mandate, the youngster who is eligible for special education services is guaranteed multidisciplinary evaluation, parent participation in program design, individually designed instruction, a lower teacher-student ratio, if needed, regular program review, and ancillary therapy services. In theory, these provisions seem to meet the needs of all youngsters with exceptionalities. In practice, existing program options rarely meet the unique needs of the child who has sustained traumatic head injury.

Eligibility requirements for special education services to these children and adolescents have been made clearer by the addition of a formalized definition of head injury (in P.L. 101-476 Individuals with Disabilities Education Act) as a handicapping condition that may require special education programming. Once deemed eligible though, the issue of program design is less clear. There are only a small number of model programs across the country designed specifically to meet the needs of the student who has sustained head injury.

The provision of an Individualized Educational Program with ancillary services would seem to address the specific needs of the student. In practice, the low incidence of such students within any single school frequently requires considerable programming creativity. Existing special education programs are typically not designed to address the kinds of cognitive retraining and compensation techniques needed by the head-injured student. The existing student teacher ratio in special education programs, although smaller than in general education classes, may not meet the need for high supervision and frequent periods of one-to-one instruction that best serve this population.

The pervasive effects of traumatic head injury often require that a wide variety of ancillary services be provided within the educational model. It would not be unusual for a child who has sustained traumatic head injury to reenter school requiring speech-language therapy, physical therapy, occupational therapy, and counseling. Students with most other exceptionalities require fewer types of support services to accommodate their educational needs. The variety and degree of therapy needed by the student returning to school following head injury will impact considerably on the design of their instructional program. It is best if ancillary therapists are readily available to the student and their teacher, and most logical that the therapy interventions take place in the natural context of classroom instruction or other school activities.

To avoid the inappropriate placement of students who have sustained traumatic head injury with children whose educational objectives are fundamentally different, the development of regional programs for the head-injured population is advocated. The design of such programs can be developed with the unique cognitive, psychomotor, and psychosocial sequelae of traumatic head injury in mind. A very small teacher-student ratio is recommended, and the total integration of ancillary services into daily activities (much like that which is strived for in some rehabilitation programs) should be a part of that design. Because language needs are prominent following head injury, a team teaching model that includes both a special education teacher and a speech-language pathologist is optimal. Strong behavioral programming and parent education components are also needed. So too is the provision for close monitoring for other possible emerging deficits such as learning, behavioral, or psychiatric disorders that can be expected for several reasons: as a factor of further development that may not proceed normally, or because of the student's reaction to their deficits as limitations become more apparent in daily activities.

Only a very few model programs exist for students who have sustained traumatic head injury, and only those school districts with sophisticated knowledge of this population recognize the necessity for specialized models. Too often, school districts try to expand existing resources to include these students, which only frustrates both the child and the professionals who are asked to provide services without sufficient education and experience with this population.

Noninstructional Barriers

In an optimal situation, much thought and teamwork enters into the instructional planning for a student returning to school following traumatic head injury; noninstructional barriers must be considered as well. For example, in a typical school day, each student encounters a wide variety of situations that might include riding public transportation or walking across well-traveled streets, changing classes, opening lockers and organizing materials, navigating the cafeteria, meeting the differing expectations of several teachers, and countless social encounters. A youngster who, because he or she has sustained head injury, has trouble interpreting conversation and facial expression, remaining focused amidst environmental stimuli, remembering details, or moving about in crowded hallways will undoubtedly meet with countless noninstructional obstacles to smooth school reintegration.

Part of the reentry process must include consideration for each noninstructional aspect of the student's school day. When such facets are not considered, the educational placement team may be undermining the youngster's school adjustment, which sometimes provokes psychiatric sequelae such as anxiety or depression.

Time of Year

The school calendar, as it exists in most jurisdictions today, was originally developed within the context of an agricultural society, leaving an extended vacation in the summer months when harvesting was most important. Many educational professionals feel that this runs counter to what we have now learned about the learning process. These educators believe that the extended vacation is detrimental to most youngsters.

Texts and journal articles on cognitive return following traumatic head injury emphasize the need for repetition, structure, and continuity (Blosser & DePompei, 1989; Sohlberg & Mateer, 1989b). This simply is not possible when the student's educational program is suspended for 10 weeks a year. During this period, families are forced to seek interim programs that, by their nature, cannot provide the continuity of services recommended by experienced clinicians and researchers. Traditional summer school programs are typically accelerated or condensed versions of a semester-long course. In that context, repetition and reduced pace are not possible. Summer remedial and recreational programs may be desirable, but do not offer the continuity and integration of services recommended for a youngster with head injury.

A small percentage of students with handicaps do receive year-round programming, but only a minuscule number by comparison with all youngsters identified with handicapping conditions. An extended school year is provided through special education services to youngsters for whom it is deemed necessary. That is, year-round instruction is provided to those who without the extended year would show regression so extreme that relearning would not be possible. Students who have sustained a recent traumatic head injury should be included in such extended school programming, especially during crucial phases of their recovery. While it is never possible to prove that a student would regress beyond recoupment without an extended school year, extended-year programming should be considered for all students who have sustained traumatic head injury, and applied whenever it is considered appropriate.

REINTEGRATION PROCESS

Currently, transition has become an important term in special education, especially for those students moving from the educational to the vocational realm. Transition plans are now a required part of many students' Individual Educational Plans. Not only must there be a plan for transition, it must be remembered that this transition is a process, not an event. So too, the process of reintegration from the hospital to the community must be seen as a continuum along which the child, family, rehabilitation professionals, and educational professionals must all play a part.

The goal of school and community reintegration following traumatic head injury is that the youngster will experience both academic and social success. Savage and Carter (1988) have outlined four components of the successful transition back to school for the student who has sustained traumatic head injury:

1. Involvement of the school-based special education team and the hospital or rehabilitation facility,
2. Inservice training for all school-based staff who will have contact with the student,
3. Short- and long-term planning for support services needed for the student, and
4. Continued follow-up by the rehabilitation professionals.

Planning for Discharge at Admission

By experience, rehabilitation facilities have learned that, although a child's outcome is uncertain, planning for discharge should begin on the day of admission. Many pediatric head trauma rehabilitation programs have developed a checklist they use to work toward smooth school reintegration. (See Figure 5-1.)

The hospital-based educational specialist or psychologist, meeting with the family on the day of admission, should obtain permission to share information regarding their child with the school system. This sets the stage for the ongoing dialogue which should exist during the rehabilitation stay and beyond.

The educator then contacts the school staff to make them aware of the child's current situation and to obtain school records containing information regarding pretraumatic social and educational functioning. Having a clear picture of pretraumatic functioning is necessary, as studies have found that a disproportionate number of children and adolescents who have sustained traumatic head injury had preexisting learning disabilities or behavioral problems (Rutter, 1981).

This initial school contact is important and serves many purposes. The first is that it begins the cooperative interaction between agencies necessary for successful reintegration into

KENNEDY KRIEGER INSTITUTE
PEDIATRIC COMPREHENSIVE NEUROREHABILITATION PROGRAM
School Reintegration Checklist

completed   date/comments

DAY OF ADMISSION
____ Family Orientation to Educational Services
____ Obtain Release for School Records
____ Initial School Contact
    ____ background data
    ____ establish contact person
    ____ arrange for books and assignments
    ____ explore school resources

EARLY ADMISSION
____ Initial Educational Screening
____ Provide School with Educational Materials on Head Injury
____ Encourage Appropriate School Participation
    (i.e. sending tapes and photos, or visiting)

MID-ADMISSION
____ Monitor Cognitive Return
____ Enroll in Daily Academic Therapy
____ Encourage Appropriate School Participation
____ Make Referrals for Outpatient Services
    (including Special Education services)
____ Plan School Visit to Assess Needs

LATE ADMISSION
____ School Staff Visit to Observe Rehab Therapy
____ Discharge Educational Evaluation
____ Disseminate Rehabilitation Reports to Referral Sources
____ Meet with School Personnel to Plan Reintegration
    ____ establish case manager
    ____ academic program
    ____ noninstructional considerations
____ Inservice School Staff
____ Inservice Peers

FOLLOWING DISCHARGE
____ School Visit or Phone Contact
____ School Program Review
____ Periodic Reevaluation
____ Additional Consultations and Training

Figure 5-1. Kennedy Krieger Institute School Reintegration Checklist.

the school and community. The rehabilitation professional should offer information regarding current functioning and prognosis, and extend an invitation to school personnel and classmates (if appropriate) to visit and participate in the rehabilitation.

It also marks the first opportunity for educating school personnel in the important aspects of traumatic brain injury and the recovery process. Each contact between educational and rehabilitation professionals is an opportunity for each to educate the other in the workings of their respective system.

In addition to obtaining data on pretraumatic functioning and beginning to educate the school regarding traumatic head injury, the initial contact should include a request for the patient's actual school books and assignments. It is most logical in rehabilitation to set up situations similar to those to which the youngster is expected to return — for this, the use of actual school materials is advantageous. Clear communication of rehabilitation status is most necessary at this time, because the request for assignments can be misinterpreted by educators and family. They might assume the student is considered competent to complete the assignments as given. Both the family and the school need to be told that the student will have reduced interaction with school assignments because of his or her current level of cognitive functioning or physical condition. When parents and teachers observe the patient's interaction with familiar materials, they become more oriented to the child's present abilities. Similarly, the rehabilitation clinician can use these observations as a part of their functional assessment and in setting pertinent discharge goals.

In early contacts between the rehabilitation facility and the educational agency, each should establish a single contact person and a means of keeping informed regularly. It is the joint responsibility of the school and the rehabilitation facility to establish contact. If a school staff is not consulted regarding one of their students, they should not hesitate to take the initiative of making the first contact. In some regions, there is already a working relationship between existing medical and educational settings. Where this is not the case, all should do their part in creating such coordination.

Lastly, the initial contacts between the rehabilitation and educational agencies serve as a beginning in planning and exploring options for discharge services. Providing some sense of prognosis allows the school to begin to make plans — sometimes exploring creative interagency options not typically used. The rehabilitation therapists will need to know what programming options exist, what physical barriers may need to be overcome, and what psychosocial supports can be available to the student and the family. With this information, the rehabilitation professionals can set more realistic discharge goals and begin to design an individualized program for their patient.

During the Rehabilitation Process

School Interaction

Throughout the weeks of rehabilitation that follow severe traumatic head injury, the reintegration plan continues. Many rehabilitation therapists find it helpful to ask that the school contact them regularly for an update on the youngster's progress. This gives the school a more active role and serves to avoid the "out of sight, out of mind" phenomenon that naturally occurs during extended absences.

Proximity of each facility to the other, as well as practicality in time availability will dictate the number of observation visits either program can be expected to make. If return to the student's previous school is desired, a representative of the rehabilitation facility should attempt to visit the school at this time. This visit will assist in determining whether the school can implement the range of services dictated by the child's projected needs. It should include consideration of both instructional and non-instructional needs in the school setting. That is, are there programmatic resources available in this setting, and are there any architectural or logistical barriers to returning to a program at this school?

At this visit or by mail during this phase of the student's recovery, the rehabilitation professionals should take the opportunity to provide the school with some written information about head trauma. This might begin with one or two written articles relevant to the sequelae following head trauma and to the issues of educational reintegration, as well as such basic books as the National Head Injury Foundation's *Educator's Manual* (Savage & Wolcott, 1988) or inservice materials such as the University of Kansas Medical Center's *Traumatic Head Injury in School Aged Children: A Training Manual for Educational Personnel* (Tyler, 1990). Dissemination of such materials at this time will allow for more knowledgeable future interactions in the design and planning of the student's program.

Lastly, a visit by school personnel to the rehabilitation setting for observation of the student during therapy can be invaluable. This will give the school a much more realistic sense of the child's potential needs and hopefully facilitate the school reentry process through predetermination of viable program options.

Family and Peer Education

While the youngster is actively engaged in a variety of rehabilitation therapies, the reintegration process proceeds with an emphasis on home and community education. Families are encouraged to participate in the rehabilitation process actively and many spend at least 1 day a week attending therapy sessions with their child or sibling. During these sessions, therapists can provide training in patient care techniques and point out landmarks of the recovery process as progress occurs. Gradually, with ongoing interaction, families gain further understanding of head injury and begin to reconcile themselves with the impact it will have on their lives. More formal family conferences may also be held at crucial points in the patient's recovery or at important junctures in family adaptation.

When a family does not have the opportunity to participate in rehabilitation on a regular basis because of physical distance from the facility or because of work and family obligations, a series of planned family conferences should be arranged. Although it is sometimes the only viable option, this method of parent education is undoubtedly less effective than active participation.

Siblings and peers are often inadvertently overlooked in the rehabilitation and reintegration process. Visitor age restrictions in some hospitals limit the interaction they can have with their injured friend or sibling — yet without information and support, children cannot be expected to reconcile themselves with what has happened. Without personal interaction, many imagine something far worse exists than the actual injury. Moreover, a sibling may experience guilt that they were not injured or resentment for the attention placed on the injured family member. Sibling adjustment is crucial to positive family relationships and the emotional health of the uninjured child. In addition, well-informed siblings and peers can also assist in helping the school and community understand and accept their injured brother, sister, or classmate.

Community Resources

In addition to education about their child's recovery and its implications, clinicians should also teach families about known community resources. The educator, in particular, should orient the family to the special education process in which they will likely find themselves involved. Families need to be made aware of other less intensive rehabilitation services available and of support groups and agencies that may be helpful for response to the variety of issues that may surface.

Referrals for educational and rehabilitation services that will be recommended after discharge from a comprehensive rehabilitation program should be made several weeks in advance. Negotiating the systems necessary to obtain services requires knowledge, patience, and persistence. It is helpful if one has previous experience with the process. Some families will find this too overwhelming a task at this stressful point in their lives; others will find some solace in doing something concrete and proactive for their family member. Rehabilitation professionals may need to establish, on a case-by-case basis, who will proceed with making the referrals for services, and to what extent the family should be expected to participate in the process.

Just Prior to and at Discharge

The timing of the steps within the reintegration process is unpredictable. On admission, the rehabilitation team sets an estimated discharge date by which time they predict the patient will have achieved the goals necessary for community reentry. These discharge dates are set based on experience with other patients and on the extent of the injury and the rate of the patient's progress to date. A definitive discharge date cannot be set, nor can one predict the patient's needs at that time. At best, the rehabilitation team, the school, and the family can keep each other informed and ready to take the steps necessary for eligibility and placement in a timely manner. Therefore, although the whole rehabilitative process is an active one, much action toward school reintegration necessarily occurs just prior to and at discharge.

Assessment and Dissemination of Reports

Ongoing evaluation of progress occurs throughout rehabilitation and recovery, but more formal evaluations generally occur nearing discharge. These multidisciplinary evaluations should summarize the patient's recovery course, establish their current levels of functioning, and make recommendations for services at discharge. Specific issues regarding the educational evaluation will follow in Chapter 6.

Dissemination of the reports to those educational, social, and medical agencies to which the student has been referred should occur as close to the discharge date as possible, to facilitate school eligibility and placement meetings — yet also give the most pertinent data. If reports are generated too much in advance of discharge, the data will not be effective in program planning because of the continued changes (recovery) taking place. Discharge evaluations should be completed when the patient has reached a level, or plateau, of highly predictable outcome.

Designing the Individual Educational Plan

Eligibility for special education services has become less of an issue with the inclusion of the definition of traumatic head injury in the public law. Thus, assuming the local educational agency will accept the evaluations performed in the rehabilitation setting (or has performed some evaluations of their own), school personnel, the family, and at least one representative of the rehabilitation team can now meet to design an appropriate educational program.

Meetings to discuss the admission, review, and dismissal of special education services are held regularly in most schools. Contacts with the school at an early point in the rehabilitative stay help to reserve a place on the agenda for the date closest to the head-injured student's anticipated discharge. Unfortunately, the acceptable timeline for eligibility and placement can be very lengthy (several months). Some school districts seem to be rigid on this issue, insisting on adherence to its timeline, but with further experience with this population, local educational agencies will begin to see the value and necessity of careful timing for successful school reintegration (if they have not already been effectively convinced of this by rehabilitation professionals).

At discharge from rehabilitation, when the Individual Educational Plan (IEP) is developed, a date must also be set for its review. Although educational agencies also have standard procedures for the timing of these reviews (usually annually), in the first year of services following traumatic head injury, such programmatic reviews should occur about every 60 days.

Because of the many aspects of traumatic head injury previously discussed, the educational plan for these students differs from those of students with most other handicapping conditions. Among the important differences are: the variety and degree of ancillary therapies needed, the necessity for more frequent review of services, the focus on process rather than content learning, the smaller student-teacher ratio, the prevalence of need for strict behavioral programming, and the focus on teaching compensatory strategies.

Formal Inservice Training

Once the student's community-based educational program has been determined, inservice training should be arranged for all professionals who will be working with the child. For a staff inexperienced in traumatic head injury, this may be rather generalized to the nature and sequelae of head injury. For those programs with staff considerably experienced with this population, the inservice training should be more specific to the resulting impairments and treatment methods found most effective for the particular student.

This is also a good time for peer training. When a youngster returns to school, many of his or her former friends drift away, sometimes because the changes they see in their recovering friend are misunderstood. For example, some children may associate speech disorders with mental retardation or labile emotions with mental illness rather than with head trauma. Formal peer inservice presentations in the school setting can serve the dual purposes of informing the audience about the sequelae of traumatic head injury and emphasizing injury prevention efforts. The patient should always be consulted before a peer inservice about the degree of specificity to be given about his or her particular case. Some patients have very strong feelings about whether or not they want such an inservice performed. Those with little insight into their deficits often reject the idea, wishing to avoid being the focus of attention.

Establishing Case Management

Many rehabilitation programs use a case management format. During rehabilitation, one therapist provides overall coordination of services and integration of techniques from therapy to therapy. On discharge from the rehabilitation program, this responsibility is often relinquished to the school. Although the design and implementation of an educational program for reentry following head injury is a multidisciplinary process, one person should be designated as the case manager for each specific student. This may be the special education classroom teacher, the school counselor, or one of the therapists. The case manager should be a person who has daily contact with the student. As the case manager, the school staff person needs to examine all aspects of the student's program, from transportation and instructional goals to social readjustment and noninstructional logistics. At each formal review, this person will be called on to provide feedback on the overall coordination of services.

The case manager should also be identified to the student as someone to whom they can turn when necessary. It is a good practice to schedule regular contacts between the student and the case manager for the first weeks and months following return to school.

One further function of the case manager is in interagency communication. For example, the family, physician, or rehabilitation therapist who is providing follow-up care can contact the school-based case manager to find out if there are any problem areas which should be addressed at the next appointment. Similarly, the school-based case manager may be in frequent contact with rehabilitation professionals or family members in the early stages of the return to school following head injury, trying to coordinate services and provide continuity of effective strategies from one setting to another.

Following Discharge

As the reintegration process continues, the active participation of the rehabilitation professionals lessens and the school-based professionals take on that active role within the educational setting. The responsibility of the case manager shifts from the rehabilitation program to the school, and both the medical and the educational models play a role in the student's continued improvement.

Reevaluation

Within the school setting informal reevaluation should be on-going. Daily assessment should be made of the effectiveness of teaching techniques and compensatory strategies for students returning following head injury. Their level of independence in the completion of academic and daily living tasks should be continually monitored.

Formal reevaluation can also be useful on a long-term basis. Yearly reevaluation by professionals familiar with the problems of traumatic head injury can help to identify the onset of new problems. For example, it is not unusual for the student returning to school following traumatic head injury to demonstrate average academic mastery levels. It is also not unusual to find that, 1 year later, these mastery levels may have improved very little. In addition to such onset of learning disabilities, psychiatric and psychosocial problems often surface sometime after the student's initial return to home and the community. These can be caused by organic conditions or by the child's reaction to the loss of abilities and friends. Formal reevaluation is the foundation for providing guidance in making programmatic adjustments to the necessary support services at home and in school.

Program Review

As has been previously mentioned, standard procedures for the regular review of an individual's special education program do not adequately serve the youngster with head injury. In the early weeks and months following return to school, the student's Individual Educational Plan should be reviewed formally at least every 60 days. In the following school year it should be reviewed approximately 30 days after the return from summer vacation and then at lengthier time intervals (perhaps twice more that school year). Besides the standard yearly review of each student's program, school personnel will probably find it prudent to continue with the additional formal review 30 days into each new school year. This serves as a sort of "troubleshooting" session for identification of logistical problems with the current year's schedule, new staff needing orientation to traumatic head injury, and/or student skills improvements or declines that may have surfaced during the summer requiring adjustment. Most importantly, the schedule for formal program review should be developed by the multidisciplinary team and documented in the student's Individual Educational Plan.

Further Training

Within the school setting, professionals experienced with the treatment of head injury are rare. Even school psychologists have received little systematic training in the area of traumatic head injury (Mira, Meck, & Tyler, 1988). Initial inservice trainings of school personnel unfamiliar with traumatic head injury typically focus on patterns of primary and secondary injury; the prominent cognitive, psychomotor, and psychosocial problems resulting from the injury; and typical patterns of recovery. This provides a frame of reference from which educational professionals can begin to design an individualized program.

Following the brain-injured student's return to school, more specific problem areas can be identified. This is the time student-specific training or technical assistance should be sought and provided. The school can turn to rehabilitation professionals for specific inservice training, but may have to adjust the information to fit into the context of an educational program. On rare occasions, an educational professional with extensive traumatic head injury experience is readily available. This person might be enlisted to observe the specific student, review the medical and educational records, interview family members and therapists, and then provide further inservice training or consultation specific to the needs of that student.

Some states and individual school districts have recognized the need for system-wide traumatic head injury inservice training. Unfortunately, many of these workshops do not reach the actual teachers and therapists who may be responsible for program development and implementation. While these efforts are viewed as positive in raising awareness of supervisors and administrators, school systems should not consider such programs as adequate preparation for staff. Training sessions specific to a particular student that include all of the school personnel with whom that student will come in contact, are also recommended for successful program development.

Exceptions

When working in the head-trauma field there are probably more exceptions than there are rules. The following topics briefly address school reintegration issues.

Mild Head Trauma

Mild head injury victims do not necessarily face a good outcome. Following a blow to the head, a child may experience no physical symptoms. These youngsters may be the most misunderstood. A typical scenario might include a day's observation (at home or in the hospital) and a subsequent return to school. Once back in school, the student will often complain of physical discomfort, sensory disturbance, memory impairment, or difficulty attending. Teachers sometimes misinterpret these behaviors as volitional acts to avoid academic tasks. Needless to say, this can result in a feeling of failure by the student and the teacher, as well as the parent.

Reintegration following mild head injury should include systematic evaluation by experienced professionals, teacher orientation and training, and the careful program development provided for youngsters with more serious injuries.

Medically Fragile

Some of the most unfortunate survivors of traumatic head injury are those who suffer such extensive physical impairment that they must depend on such medical interventions as tracheostomy for respiration or tube feeding for sustenance. Such medically fragile student situations pose school access issues, whatever the disability etiology. Obviously, staff trained in the necessary medical support procedures will have to be available. Also, creative programming will need to be implemented to develop a meaningful educational program for many of these severely disabled and medically fragile youngsters.

Preschoolers

In 1986, the Education for All Handicapped Children Act of 1975 (P.L. 94-142) was amended with P.L. 99-457, the Education of the Handicapped Amendments of 1986. One of the most important outcomes of these amendments was the lowering of the eligibility age for special education and related services to 3 years old. This was to have been implemented by the 1991-1992 school year. The law also established the handicapped Infants and Toddlers Program (Part H). Within this program, families may receive services that are needed to help them assist in the development of their child. State guidelines vary, but each state must have a comprehensive interagency service delivery system in place by the fifth year of participation in the program.

Within the context of these programs, preschoolers who have sustained traumatic head injury are entitled to the range of services necessary for their families to assist them in their development. In these cases, interagency coordination should include the services of rehabilitation professionals to assist in program design and to participate in the evaluation process.

The role of the case manager is very important for the preschool age group, as many children are not provided services within the context of a comprehensive school program, but instead receive appropriate care from a variety of agencies. Also, increased family education needs to be emphasized for preschoolers, infants, and toddlers. Caregivers are provided with instruction for promoting their child's independence in daily living activities and for facilitating cognitive and language development. Education in the techniques and strategies recommended for enhancing their child's development, as well as continued education in the effects of head trauma on the child's ongoing development, are necessary for both the families and other active participants in the educational program of the young brain-injured child.

Chapter 6

Educational Assessment

Assessment in the rehabilitation setting is ongoing and integrated with treatment to both evaluate efficacy of techniques and monitor ongoing progress and recovery. When a head-injured child or adolescent is about to reenter a school setting, a more formal and multifaceted evaluation must be obtained. This should be a multidisciplinary evaluation that is performed at an optimal time, is sensitive to the domains frequently affected by head injury, and that examines areas integral to school performance both formally and informally.

The educational staff is unlikely to be helped much by the results of intelligence or achievement tests given to head-injured students during the earliest period of recovery. Performance at that time is so variable, and the interaction of the deficits so unpredictable that interpretation of the scores is rendered very tentatively. Yet those scores are sometimes presented at planning conferences; although performance on such tests reflects damage, scores sometimes form a poor foundation on which to plan. It is also necessary to consider a qualitative measure to more clearly perceive the behavior and needs of students with head injury. A continuum of deficits, with an accompanying continuum of responses to the deficits is given in Table 6-1, for use in determining a student's qualitative performance within a range of behaviors. All findings should

Table 6-1. Continuum of deficits

THINKING

Easily distracted; loses train of thought; focuses poorly; looks "blank"; thinks very concretely, literally; has poor attention	Has difficulty coming to a point organizing thoughts, and categorizing	Shows poor abstraction, especially in language (e.g., proverbs), inference, drawing conclusions; unable to consolidate

READING SPEED, COMPREHENSION

Reads very slowly with comprehension well below grade level	Reads at moderate speed; identifies single words at grade level, but comprehends at least two grades below	May comprehend close to grade level but speed is slow enough to penalize

MATH: FACTS AND APPLICATION

Has poor memory for facts and processes; shows poor application and understanding of language in word problems; very confused	Exhibits fair application but poor memory for facts; may recall facts but forgets processes; has partial recall	Displays poor abstract reasoning in word problems; evidences distaste and frustration with processes such as long division with three divisors

WRITING: SPEED, LEGIBILITY

Does not write at all; cannot use writing efficiently; may be able to learn to type	Writes too slowly for preparation of work; has poor fine-motor dexterity; may have apraxia	Demonstrates moderate speed but poor legibility

AUDITORY PROCESSING

Processes spoken language very inadequately; comprehends below grade and age level; unable to follow oral directions, even in one-to-one communication	Improved one-to-one communication; markedly deficient in oral language comprehsion	Easily overloaded by amounts of oral information usually well presented during classroom instructions

VISUAL AND PERCEPTUAL ORGANIZATION

Suffers from field cuts, blurred vision, and poor depth perception	Lacks spatial organization (e.g., has difficulty lining up figures, columns in math, and so on)	Plans use of space poorly, (e.g., on paper)

JUDGMENT

Careless about safety; impulsive	Very easily persuaded by others; interacts inappropriately	Drives too soon; engages in physical activity too soon; uses alcohol and drugs

MOTIVATION

Very dependent on others to plan, to engage in activity; exhibits truancy or high absenteeism	Less dependent but less compliant for expected behaviors (e.g., attending class, completing work)	Lacking initiative

Table 6-1. Continuum of deficits (continued)

SELF-CONTROL

Overtly disinhibited, (e.g., incidents of masturbation, stealing food, profanity, aggressive behavior, inappropriate affection); emotionally labile	Moderately disinhibited; jokes inappropriately; crude; socially familiar; overactive, outspoken, talkative; loses temper	Rude; silly; appears immature for age group; is immature; verbally aggressive; sometimes escalates to fighting

SELF-MONITORING

Dresses carelessly; shows poor hygiene	Perseverative: has tics, mannerisms, repeats same phrases, gets "stuck"	Reads social and nonverbal cues or others; responds poorly; preoccupied with minor problems

MOOD AND SELF-ESTEEM

Has low affect; emotionally labile; little awareness of self	Depressed (sad/fatigued); reduced energy; aware of handicap; show perplexibility; avoids public places; irritable	Sometimes suicidal; sometimes manic; unwilling to venture out; exhibits self-doubt; hesitant

COMPLIANCE

Demonstrates outright refusal; responds with verbal outburst or physical aggression to requests or demands; runs away; is truant	Argumentative; covers up noncompliance; pretends innocence, confusion; is truant from some classes	Manipulative; noncompliant in effect but more subtle; no overt refusal but requests are not met

be conceptualized along a continuum of recovery and growth on which a student can be located. Each stage is incremental and implies improvement over previous stages, although, as in any stage theory, individuals occasionally exhibit behaviors that overlap. When using this type of chart there are some considerations:

- These are only the most common behaviors witnessed in the early stages of recovery in children and adolescents. Others may be present.
- They may be temporary, but in the meantime they are too urgent to be ignored.
- Not every student begins at the lowest point and improves; some enter midway.

MULTIDISCIPLINARY EVALUATION

Eligibility for special education services requires the completion of a multidisciplinary evaluation. This approach was designed to provide for corroboration and to reduce misidentification of handicapping conditions. This provision is especially important in program planning and design for the head-injured child. Disciplines necessary for such a multifaceted assessment might include psychology, speech-language pathology, special education, occupational therapy, physical therapy, and social work.

Rehabilitation professionals often take a neuropsychological approach, which implies the study of brain-behavior relationships and assumes a causal association between the two variables. That is, neuropsychology addresses problems in learning that are related to cerebral impairments. Although this model has emerged in the educational system in evaluating some handicapping conditions, it is not prevalent. Such an approach is often criticized as lacking in its assessment of practical skills.

Many components of the well-known neuropsychological batteries are presented in a thorough multidisciplinary evaluation. There will undoubtedly be some overlap of domains addressed, but this will provide for a necessary examination of each domain as it affects differing aspects of the child's functioning. For example, an occupational therapist may analyze visual-perceptual skills as they impact on handwriting or the performance of activities of daily living; an educator may assess the same area in relation to reading or the processing of visual stimuli for academic tasks. Communication among professionals and coordination of their respective evaluations is important, so that test-retest effect can be avoided. Similarly, communication between the rehabilitation professionals and the educational professionals will assist in determining which evaluations have been done and what others might be necessary for designing an appropriate educational plan.

Timing

Because recovery from head injury is a dynamic process, the timing of evaluations used to plan educational reintegration is an important consideration. Professionals who specialize in the assessment of this population constantly struggle with this scheduling issue and there seems to be no established guideline.

In general, assessments should be completed as close as possible to the anticipated date of school reentry. In this case, it is assumed that the school reentry has been planned for a time when the child is no longer experiencing rapid recovery of function. This puts pressure on the multidisciplinary team to complete evaluations and interpretation, meet to design an educational program, and arrange for its implementation, within a short time period. If well-planned and coordinated between the respective agencies, this is possible.

Other issues dictate the need for continuing reevaluation. Again, because recovery from head injury is dynamic and relatively long term (1–2 years), most experts agree that ongoing reevaluation is necessary to modify treatment plans. This may be especially true in an educational setting. Reevaluation, either formal or informal, should be ongoing and adjustments made to the child's Individual Educational Plan accordingly.

Some areas of difficulty do not emerge until a child or adolescent has returned to the community. It is unclear whether this is caused by late onset, or whether this behavior could not be adequately observed in the rehabilitation setting. In reality, there is probably some overlap of both phenomena. Emergence of such new problems supports the need for periodic ongoing assessment.

Lastly, developmental issues necessitate ongoing assessment. In the case of developmental disabilities, one can often predict academic progress from the previous rate of mastery. This is not the case in head injury. Pretraumatic academic levels are sometimes maintained, but significant difficulties often emerge in the learning of new tasks. Depending on the age at onset of the injury, continuing brain development also complicates the process of predicting success. Consequently, students may be functioning adequately at one stage of assessment and present problems in functioning at a later date.

DOMAINS OF IMPORTANCE

Many experts in neuropsychological assessment have identified crucial domains for investigation. Telzrow (1991) provides a review. Common among most of them are:

- Intelligence
- Attention/concentration
- Organizational skills
- Language comprehension and expression
- Judgment and reasoning
- Academic achievement
- Personality/adjustment
- Memory and learning
- Rate of information processing
- Sensory and perceptual functioning
- Motor and psychomotor functioning
- Orientation

The task of the educational team members is to choose assessment instruments which examine these domains within their area of expertise.

The educational portion of a multidisciplinary evaluation traditionally assesses academic mastery, learning style, and school performance in comparison to a normative group. Those cognitive and behavioral domains identified as pertinent to head injury may not be tapped in the standard educational battery, and, thus, the educator needs to customize an appropriate battery for these students. Many authors have identified specific instruments and instrument subtests that assess the domains of interest in evaluating the youngster with head injury. The reader is referred to such authors as Lehr (1991), Reitan (1969), Solberg and Mateer (1989a), and Telzrow (1991), for examples of suggested instruments.

Physical Factors

Many physical factors need to be considered in the selection and administration of test instruments for the head-injured child or adolescent. The most obvious is stamina. Fatigue and headaches are common following head injury and should be considered not only when making plans for school reintegration, but during the evaluation process as well. Actual testing should be broken into several sessions, the length being dictated by the student's needs. Members of the multidisciplinary assessment team should also coordinate and time sessions so as not to overfatigue or overwhelm the student.

The head-injured child's ability to gain, sustain, and shift attention should also be considered in evaluation. Although clinical observations of the student's ability to attend and shift attention will be valuable to program planning, it may be necessary to vary the tasks within each session to obtain optimal testing results.

Sensorimotor impairment following head injury may also impact on the selection of instruments. For example, visual field defects are common following head trauma. This puts rather obvious limits on instrument selection, and may dictate the need for adapting the visual stimuli presentation by altering the location (e.g., to one side) or enlarging printed material. Similarly, difficulty in verbal expression may dictate the need for a multiple-choice test format in assessing areas of academic mastery. The examiner should first attempt to choose instruments that can be administered as standardized. While any alterations in standard procedures must be described in the written report, and scores should be interpreted cautiously, much information regarding a student's approach to a task and suspected functioning in an educational setting can be observed by making only small adaptations.

Most formalized test manuals offer suggestions for standard administration of assessment in a quiet distraction-free environment. As children and adolescents who have sustained head injury frequently tend to display impulsivity and distractibility, this factor is of great importance. In adapting the environment, the evaluator must realize he or she may have obtained results of learning potential that will not be duplicated when the youngster faces such tasks in the typical classroom environment with its inherent distractions.

Informal Naturalistic Samples

As mentioned previously, use of formal assessment for program design means samples of performance are taken in highly structured, artificial situations. Therefore, formal testing, by its nature, compensates for many debilitating executive impairments, which can be caused by head injuries. To investigate such areas as new learning potential and capacity for orientation to a classroom environment, educators must add naturalistic assessments to their standardized batteries. Traits such as self-awareness, realistic goal-setting, organization, motivation, and initiation may be overlooked in a traditional educational assessment, yet these executive functions are necessary for success in most educational settings.

Observation and interview are two means of investigating traits such as those listed above. Observations, although ecologic, should not be random. Facets which require systematic consideration in the context of an observation are: parameters of the task, environmental factors, guidelines for assessing the quality or quantity of the behavior, and the degree of cuing and compensation required to complete the task. Because so many variables are important in interpreting observations, several samples of behavior should be conducted.

Interviews with family members or professionals active in the head-injured child's treatment will enhance information on the student's function in a natural environment, and usually identify problems not noted in formal testing. Areas of interest in this type of interview might include: attention length and quality, flexibility in thinking and in shifting attention, use of compensatory strategies, insight into deficits, potential for new learning, response to stress, initiation skills, judgment, and problem-solving ability. Information obtained through observation and interview may also help the examiner select a formal test instrument to attempt to more clearly define an area of difficulty.

Previous Functioning

Much of the research in the area of cognitive outcome of head-injured students looks at within and between group comparisons without normal controls. For a review of this research, see Goldstein and Levin (1985). These research findings have allowed some prediction of outcome across levels of injury severity, but have shed little light on assessment of the return to "normal" functioning. To assess a child's functioning in reference to his or her "normal" functioning, the examiner needs to possess an accurate picture of pretraumatic functioning.

Comparing a student with himself or herself, pre- and posttraumatically, should best inform educational professionals of those adaptations necessary for success within general or special education programming. Test scores that place a student's behavior and mastery as within normal limits may not appear to be problematic. However, study habits developed prior to head trauma may not be adequate for success posttraumatically. In this case, the student will be subjected to unexplained failure. Any alteration in functioning needs to be identified and addressed in the educational plans.

Prior school records are the most obvious source for documentation of pretraumatic school functioning. Most school-age youngsters are routinely given standardized group achievement batteries yielding comparisons with age or grade peers. Students who have been previously identified with handicapping conditions must have individualized intelligence or achievement data available in their educational record. This information should be analyzed to provide a frame of reference for the youngster's recovery.

As other neurobehavioral factors also impact on school performance following head injury, it is helpful to acquire pre- and posttraumatic behavioral inventories. Family members and former teachers should be interviewed and asked to complete formal surveys on pretraumatic functioning. This should be done as soon as possible following the injury, because this information is subjective in nature, and many youngsters tend to be remembered only at their best in such an emotionally charged situation as the crisis of serious injury. Such surveys might identify pretraumatic attention deficit disorder, learning problems, conduct disorders, or emotional problems. Knowledge of such preexisting problems will alter interpretation of current evaluation findings and program goals.

Interpretation

In interpreting test findings, it is most important to note that most of the instruments in use are not normed for students with head injury. Findings provide guidance for academic placement and preferred strategies, but cannot be considered definitive.

Academic achievement batteries measure mastery or prior learning. In the general population, the student's rate of mastery allows educational professionals to predict his or her continued rate of progress. Such is not the case following head trauma. Some solace can be taken in that much academic mastery is so overlearned that it either remains intact or is regained quickly following head injury. Retained skills in the encoding and decoding of language, as well as the ability to follow mathematics processes, and the knowledge of factual information in content areas are important, but less so if skills cannot be utilized effectively to enhance new learning. Thus, scores that place students at various academic levels are valuable only in identifying appropriate units of study. Methods of instruction, necessary compensatory strategies, behavioral strategies, and environmental adaptations need to be ascertained from the results of a variety of other subtests, interviews, and clinical observations.

Inconsistent performance is also a hallmark of head injury. It is not unusual to note, for example, that a student who has sustained head trauma can perform problems of multiplication, but he or she can also make errors on some of the simplest of problems of addition or subtraction. This variability is important to note not only in test interpretation, but also in administration. The standard practice employed by most individually administered instruments of establishing a basal and a ceiling can lead to erroneous results. Evaluators are encouraged to administer tests such as these in the standard manner, and then to continue to test both upward and downward for additional information.

Another prevalent problem following head trauma is reduced efficiency in many cognitive and sensorimotor functions. Often a student can respond without errors, but at a rate that would penalize him or her in an academic setting. Administration of both timed and untimed tests can assist in quantifying what the examiner has observed clinically. Failure to identify such inefficiencies often leads to unexplained difficulty in the school setting that is misinterpreted as a lack of motivation or a conduct disorder, when, in reality, it is related to organic brain damage.

Scores on any subtest of the multidisciplinary evaluation should not be interpreted without close clinical assessment of the meaning and implications of the results. For example, poor performance on a verbal reasoning task may be due to word retrieval difficulties rather than verbal reasoning. Low scores on a multiple-choice format test of reading or mathematics achievement may be caused by an undiagnosed visual field deficit that prevented the student from adequately viewing all of the response choices. Subtests designed to assess memory or executive function may yield poor results because of the student's poor attentional status or tendency toward impulsivity. Although all of these results are valuable in the overall assessment, the multidisciplinary team must be careful to report findings in light of the many factors that may enter into the assessment of the head-injured child or adolescent.

SUMMARY

In evaluation and interpretation of findings of the multidisciplinary assessment of a student who has experienced head trauma, the educational team must consider the impact of the injury on all aspects of the student's behavior. They need to consider the implications of its sudden and late onset, and they should assess areas of importance to both academic and non-academic school functioning. Each finding should be analyzed in light of what it purports to measure, but should also be task analyzed to examine whether the difficulty lies in a component or precursor skill. It is important to keep in mind the broad range of head injury sequelae, the pretraumatic skills of the student, and the unique set of strengths and needs that each student who has experienced head injury is likely to manifest.

Chapter 7

Instructional Strategies

CLASSROOM APPLICATION

Preparation

By now, teachers and parents should have a good sense of the person who is recovering from head trauma and some idea of the problems that person will present as a student. As a teacher, the best way to prepare for the entry into your class of a student who has sustained head trauma is to be well informed. You will need information and orientation regarding head trauma and, in particular, your student. Still, how do teachers prepare for the demands that the student who has sustained head injury will make on them?

First, teachers must accept the student's placement in their classrooms.

Often teachers have little to say about whom is assigned to their classes. But, strong feelings about the task of managing a very difficult child need to be acknowledged. The experience of one of the authors has been that many teachers can identify with the unfortunate circumstances of severe injury and give their best. As time passes and the teacher is confronted daily with the challenges of such students, this empathy can become more difficult to muster. Although, for the most part, teachers can expect continued spontaneous improvements following initial reintegration from the hospital, they must also be prepared for the later onset of further problems as the student is confronted with new challenges.

> Not all head-injured students present enormous problems, but a few are very trying and require patience, ingenuity, and perseverance nearly beyond the expectations of a teacher's job duties.

Sometimes teachers need to be allowed to step back from the situation to gain perspective or to seek advice. This is a time when they should be able to count on support from the school administrators and other staff members. Some support needs to take the form of released time for courses and workshops, plus consultations with others who can advise and assist. The reality is that not all students with head injury are likable, and some students who have sustained head trauma are less likable than others.

Review vs. New Learning

Educators are accustomed to conceptualizing learning as a hierarchical process in which one thing builds on another, and skills at a basic level are taught and learned before going on to more advanced skills and concepts. We must view the student who has experienced head injury in a different framework. Having previously been amidst the normal cumulative process of learning, the child or adolescent who has experienced head injury has a sudden interruption of their cognitive functioning. Severe injuries present with the partial shutdown of the central nervous system. Once alert, the student will experience inefficient thinking as the result of memory, attentional, sensory, cognitive, or integration impairments. As has been discussed in the previous chapter, it is not unusual to see scatter and variability in academic skills following head injury. The teacher is now presented with the task of reviewing previously learned material and promoting new learning.

In reteaching previously known skills, it is important to start at a very basic level. For example, a student may be able to conceptually solve an applied mathematics problem, but he or she may no longer recall some of the basic mathematics calculation facts. Although the student may be offended by a return to material he or she perceives as suitable for a younger student, the need for review should be explained to the student as a part of the recovery process. Similarly, retention from day-to-day should not be assumed. Overlearning, or repeated drill and study to increase the length of time something will be remembered, does not have the same value for the review of previously learned information as it typically does in new learning. Such repetition can serve as an assessment of the student's progress in relearning.

New learning is quite another matter. Not all students with head injuries exhibit all deficits, but presented deficits form unique clusters. Depending on the site of the injury and the extent of secondary injury, any number and combination of cognitive, sensory, and communicative deficits may occur. Teachers must develop an awareness of their student's strengths and weaknesses and respond to them via optimal teaching methods if they hope to achieve new learning. Depending on the objective of the lesson, the teacher may want to concentrate on remediating the student's weaknesses, or, at other times, circumventing deficits. For example, if the objective is to promote the acquisition of content information, then the teacher should optimize the student's chances of understanding the information by presenting it via the student's strongest processing modality. An information processing model offers a simple guide to teachers in analyzing their student's strengths and needs.

The first step in the process is gathering information. The teacher may examine such areas as attention, initiation, or preferred sensory input. Next, the student needs to retain the information. Here the educator may need to evaluate relative strengths among the various types of memory: immediate, short-term, long-term, episodic, rote, or semantic. Finally, retrieval is the last step of the model. Probably the most difficult to assess, retrieval may involve internal organization and reasoning, and it is influenced by preferred output modalities.

In facing the challenges of helping a student acquire new learning, it is also important that the parents be informed and involved. Watching the reacquisition of previously known academic skills can, understandably, promote optimism on the part of the family that things are returning to normal. Frequently, the parents of a head-injured child have not yet reconciled themselves fully to the idea that their child may exhibit further difficulties, even if the youngster reaches his or her pretraumatic achievement status.

Instructional Strategies

The remainder of this chapter will suggest and outline some more specific instructional strategies to be applied for this population. Skilled and intuitive teachers will find none of them new, especially if trained in the field of special education. In general, professionals should take more of a process approach in the instruction of persons who have sustained head injury. This follows from the logic that one or more of the cognitive processes have been impaired by the brain injury, and thus need to be remediated or circumvented.

In the first year of recovery, remediation should be the focus, but teachers need not be relentless. For the sake of continued progress and the self-esteem of the student with head injury, there needs to be a balance between working on the more frustrating task of remediation and using compensatory strategies.

The suggestions that follow are drawn from the author's experience and the publications of other professionals, such as Adamovich and Henderson (1990) and Rhein and Farmer (1991). The methods are far from exhaustive, yet are aimed at providing activities both for remediation and compensation.

Attention

It is usually not difficult to recognize students who have difficulty with attention and distractibility. In fact, the experience of one of the authors is that when providing descriptive information to school staff regarding a student's attentional difficulties, school staff liken these difficulties to those of many other students. If a head-injured student had attentional problems pretraumatically, these difficulties will likely be exacerbated. Students with head injury may also experience a sort of "internal distractibility," appearing to be attentive, but, through no fault of their own, concentration is diverted by his or her own thoughts. Some familiar techniques to use to increase and sustain attention are:

- Limit competing distractions in the environment and gradually introduce distractions as attentional skills improve.
- Provide the student with preferential seating near the teacher, chalkboard, or lab table.
- Assign the student to work in a small group setting, such as a special education classroom.
- Limit the length or intensity of the instructional session, gradually increasing demands as attentional skills increase.
- Use techniques that focus attention, such as prefacing important instructions as such, touching the student subtly on the shoulder, or gaining eye contact.
- Set up a personalized cuing system with the student to encourage self-monitoring. It is not necessary to stigmatize the student by continually calling his or her name to gain attention; instead, develop a less intrusive sign to let the student know that he or she appears to be inattentive.
- Gain attention with meaningful stimuli. Teach from a point of familiarity, then moving on to new or less familiar concepts.

Orientation

Patients usually experience moderate-to-severe disorientation as they emerge from coma. This period of disorientation has already been described as posttraumatic amnesia. By the time most students return to school, the severe orientation problems have been resolved. Some students may be confused about finding their way around a building, particularly if it is a new building for that student. Other students may experience periods of disorientation, especially in more stressful situations. Strategies might include:

- Assign a student or staff member as a buddy to accompany the student from class to class. Lasting disorientation is rare, although some students with head injury may have persistent problems with short-term memory and visual-spatial orientation.

- Teach the student very specific strategies to carry out when they become disoriented.
- Provide orienting cues such as "I will see you in class tomorrow, Tom; it is time for you to go to Mr. Green's math class."
- Memory and orientation are inherently linked. The use of compensatory strategies for memory should also assist in resolving disorientation.

Information Processing

Information processing is, in essence, the registration of sensory information and should lead to storage for future use. Some general hints for enhancing information processing are offered next. More specific strategies for various sensory impairments follow.

- Begin with meaningful, preferred, or more emotionally charged information to increase the likelihood of gaining attention and facilitating sensory intake.
- Determine the strongest method of information processing for each student, i.e. simultaneous, sequential, visual, auditory, or tactile.
- Determine the amount of information that the student can process in one period of time. Shorten chunks of information given and gradually increase the demands as skills improve.

Sensory Perception

Auditory

The most common sensory impairments that affect academic functioning are auditory and visual. Because auditory perception is an integral part of overall cognitive functioning, head-injured students may have unstable abilities in comprehending spoken language, and, therefore, face varying difficulty in tracking oral instructions given in the classroom. Component parts of perception are attention, memory, and processing, and some degree of deficit in this area is present in most patients, if only temporarily. It is common for a secondary student who has experienced head injury to return to school with auditory comprehension comparable to that of an elementary student. Some recommended strategies are:

- Teacher's directions should be simplified, reworded, and repeated.
- Instruction should be provided in a multisensory format.
- Ask the student to repeat what is understood and clarify this feedback as necessary.
- Clarification of instructions can be enhanced with examples the student is familiar with.
- Provide speech-language therapy to remediate specific auditory processing deficits.

Visual

Double vision and visual field cuts, including hemianopsia, are all possible outcomes of head injury. Teachers should look through the medical record for indication of these problems or ask the family or the student if they are present. As with many sequelae, these visual deficits usually resolve to some degree, but are also subject to compensation by the student. Some additional strategies might include:

- Preferential seating. For example, a student with a right field cut should be seated on the right side of the room, so that most of what is viewed is to his or her left.
- Color cue printed material. For example, a student with a left field cut often begins to read in the middle of the line. Color cue the beginning of the sentence and instruct the student to turn his or her head to scan to the left until seeing the color cue before beginning to read each line.
- Positioning of reading and instructional material should be optimized. Some patients have difficulty viewing the lower field of vision. These students may be seen lowering their head to view the material through their upper field.

Students will be more physically comfortable if the material is elevated on an easel.
- Provide visual material that is simplified and free from unnecessary distractors.
- Encourage the student to use a ruler or other external guide to aid visual scanning.
- Incorporate frequent visual rest breaks.
- Monitor the student individually during visually based activities to ensure that all pertinent information can be viewed and is included.
- Provide occupational therapy as a related service to work on specific objectives to remediate visual-perceptual deficits.

Comprehension

Reading

Even as decoding, reading fluency, and word attack improve, reading comprehension, a more complex process, may remain several grade levels below the other reading skills. Resource assistance is usually required. In either the resource room or the general education classroom the following methods might be employed:

- Provide the student with the same content material, rewritten to his or her level of reading comprehension.
- Allow the student to listen to audiotapes of reading material as the youngster reads.
- Have the student restate the ideas of the author in his or her own words. This can be done both orally and in writing, providing a written record for the student's reference and allowing the teacher to monitor whether or not essential ideas have been understood.
- Prior to the reading of the material, present the student with an outline or overview, highlighting key terms and relationships in the passage. This may be more applicable for a content area such as science than it would be for literature.
- Focus and direct the student's attention to salient points

using a Directed Thinking and Reading Activity (DTRA). This method has the unique characteristic of drawing on prior knowledge that may be more accessible than drawing on more recently learned information.

- Teach study skills such as outlining, highlighting, and key-word notetaking when most applicable.

Mathematics

Variable patterns are noted in the recovery of mathematics skills by head-injured students. Whereas some patients seem to recover math reasoning, but cannot recall basic calculation facts, others relearn the overlearned facts quickly and are left with deficits in comprehension of mathematic concepts. In the latter case a teacher might:

- Use manipulative items to demonstrate mathematics concepts, gradually fading tools as concepts are internalized.
- Allow the use of a calculator so that the student can focus on problem-solving rather than calculation.
- Incorporate methods typically employed in reading comprehension when the approaches can be applied to the language of mathematics. For example, teach the student to highlight key words such as "of," "into," "altogether," and "difference" for their mathematical meaning.
- Provide activities which translate word problems into equations and ones that require the student to make up word problems that correspond to numerical equations.
- Encourage family members to integrate the application of mathematics to everyday functioning in such activities as shopping, cooking, and scheduling family events.

Listening

In contrast to auditory perception, listening comprehension refers to the conceptual understanding of material provided auditorily. It is, in effect, the end product of auditory processing.

Assuming no impairment in auditory perception and processing, the following suggestions are offered for auditory comprehension of information in a lecture format or the following of oral directions:

- Adapt any of the reading comprehension strategies to the auditory format. For example, have the student retell the story or material that he or she has heard.
- Gradually incorporate lengthier listening exercises within each instructional content area.
- Allow the student to have written scripts of lectures to compensate for reduced auditory comprehension.
- Allow note-taking or assign a note-taker for lectures.
- Give oral directions more than once.
- Combine oral directions with visual cues.

Organization

Impairment in a student's ability to organize thoughts and actions is pervasive in its effect on all aspects of functioning. In an educational setting, students need to be able to systematize themselves to accomplish activities such as writing papers, taking notes, completing assignments on time, and being prepared in class. Suggestions to enhance organizational skills are:

- Provide organization by breaking the assignment into steps.
- Teach the student to outline important points before answering a question.
- Teach the student to ask him- or herself cuing "wh" type questions.
- Provide activities in content area instruction that focus on such skills as categorization (inclusion and exclusion characteristics) or task analysis.
- Set up external organization aids such as a notebook, assignment sheet, calendar, and locker organization. Assign a case manager to daily monitor their use.
- Provide activities which require the proper sequencing of steps of an activity. Use pertinent functional activities.

Memory

Although many survivors of head injury lack insight into their deficits, memory deficits tend to be recognized and acknowledged; memory impairment is probably the most frequently cited sequela of head injury. This may be attributed to the fact that so many precursor skills such as processing, organization, storage, and retrieval are a part of what we call memory, and problems with any one of these functions will affect what is recalled. Strategies to improve overall memory must follow remediations or compensations of the precursor skills. There are numerous mnemonic strategies, but head-injured students should be acquainted with only a few versatile strategies that can be applied to a variety of settings. They will likely adopt those they find most applicable and least cumbersome. Memory strategies may be internal or external. Specific recall strategies might include:

- Require the student to provide a verbal description of the concept or fact to be remembered. If he or she cannot do so adequately, then the description can be provided by the teacher. Explanations and descriptions should be well developed and may touch on visual, auditory, or semantic aspects of the idea.
- Encourage the student to mentally picture (visual imagery) events, objects, scenes of a story, or physical layouts.
- Teach chunking activities where information is organized into portions commensurate with the student's memory span.
- Teach the student to organize information into categories to make recall easier.
- Use verbal rehearsal. Encourage the student to repeat information aloud, subvocally, and finally to themselves.
- Have the student develop associations. For example, a student may remember a friend's name, Julie, because she wears lots of jewelry; the two words are associated both acoustically and semantically.
- Help the student to link events to be recalled with those that occurred at a similar point in time.

- Teach the student to use study strategies such as SQ3R (survey, question, read, recite, and review).
- Develop outlining and notetaking skills.
- Require the use of a daily notebook organizer where the student can record all assignments, refer to his or her schedule, refer to notes or assignments, and centrally locate all necessary information.

Reasoning and Mental Flexibility

Flexibility of thinking is taken for granted in the average youngster. Teaching methods classes given at universities to prospective teachers rarely focus on this prominent need of the student with head injury. Considerations include:

- Recognize that a rephrased question, for example, on a test, will likely be perceived as a new question and that the student may claim a lack of familiarity with it. If your intention is to test the student's knowledge of the facts, state the question as studied.
- Provide instruction that does not require high degrees of assimilation. That is, focus on one topic or aspect of a concept before going on to interrelate it with others.
- Practice reasoning tasks, such as exercises in analyzing facts. For example, when two facts are necessary to reach a conclusion, provide one fact and let the student choose the second fact that will lead to the conclusion.
- Provide activities such as crossword puzzles.
- Role play cause-and-effect scenarios.
- Provide wh-question activities (to facilitate reasoning) such as: Why do cars need gas? or What should you do if you have to be at school, but you miss the bus?
- Provide exercises in the comprehension of figurative language, such as idioms, or the multiple meanings of homonyms. By the same token, the teacher should realize that idioms and figurative language will cause confusion when not directly taught or explained.
- Role play mediating an argument. Two points of view are provided and the student is asked to analyze and synthesize the information, then arrive at a solution acceptable to both parties.

- Provide speech-language therapy with direct goals to optimize functioning in this area.

Independent Functioning

The frontal lobes are especially susceptible to damage from head injury. Research and experience working with clients who have sustained head injury have led to the description of a behavior pattern referred to as the frontal lobe syndrome. The behaviors include a mixture of behavioral and emotional deficits, as well as difficulty with executive functions. Executive functions are activities related to goal completion, such as anticipation, selection, planning, initiation, self-monitoring, and using feedback to change behavior. Students with impairment in executive functioning may have normal scores on IQ tests and other psychologic measures. Intellectual skills may remain intact, but the child or adolescent can still be dysfunctional and dependent because of deficits in executive functioning. Some suggestions are:

- The teacher must complete a careful task analysis of each assignment given. The student may need to be provided with an external checklist or outline.
- The student may also need cuing for initiation of each step of a process. Such cues should be provided and then faded to more subtle cues until prompts can be faded altogether.
- Establish routines for the completion of regular tasks.
- Establish self-monitoring cues for the student to take on the compensation strategies him- or herself.
- Each task or assignment should serve as a vehicle for practice of executive functioning. The teacher should gradually expect the student to become more independent.

Speed and Accuracy

Some students will return to school with no ability to write. A permanent weakness, or ataxia, of their dominant hand may require that such students learn to switch dominance. It is

important to appreciate the time and effort expended to complete typical academic assignments under this condition. Think
about how long it might take to learn to use a nondominant
hand skillfully enough to take notes in a lecture. Imagine the
student's dilemma when an assignment is put on the board a
few minutes before the class is to end. Add to that the tension
of trying to copy information before an early dismissal from
class, which is necessary so the student can reach his or her
next class on time. The types of deficits seen in speed and
accuracy of handwriting can surface for cognitive functions as
well. Guidelines for both include:

- Eliminate unnecessary tasks, such as copying work from
  the board, by allowing the student to have a carbon copy
  of another student's transcription.
- Have the student practice taking notes from a lecture, but
  subsequently allow them to use a teacher's study guide.
- Refer the student for the prescription of assistive technology. Portable computers with adapted access can be
  useful not only for speed and accuracy, but also for such
  other needs as organization information storage.
- Do not require the student to work under timed conditions.
- Schedule a class period providing the student with the
  opportunity to go back and finish assignments from other
  classes.
- Give oral tests, multiple-choice, or short-answer activities.
- Allow a latency period. That is, give the student time to
  respond before cuing or going on to another student for
  the answer. If necessary, provide cues for the initiation
  of a response.

Conduct

Many aspects of a student's conduct can be affected by head
injury. Difficulties in self-control, compliance, motivation,
mood, or self-esteem may need to be addressed.

As patients emerge from coma they frequently exhibit an
extreme form of self-control loss. It is referred to as disinhibition.
Disinhibited patients may swear a lot, they may masturbate

publicly, they are often agitated and sometimes aggressive. It is unlikely that they will return to school with such extreme behaviors, but some degree of disinhibition may remain.

Lack of control may also show up in inappropriate crudeness or joking, or in instances of uncontrollable laughter or tears. Even when it is understood that such behaviors are not volitional, it is a challenge for the classroom teacher to manage the behavior while trying to maintain classroom control.

One specific behavior that may persist is overeating. This hyperphagia can lead to food stealing and obesity. As the patient regains self-control, the hyperphagia becomes more manageable. One patient's family reports having to place locks on the refrigerator and cupboards to safeguard against food stealing and overeating during the middle of the night. This child's teachers reported that 3 years after the accident the student was still first at the table whenever there was a social function. Still, there was progress toward self-control.

Other forms of disinhibition show up in social interactions. For example, one 17-year-old patient spoke to everyone in the elevator indiscriminately and approached people on the street by introducing himself. A 16-year-old girl hugged people inappropriately. One 5-year-old boy kissed the hand of everyone he came into contact with. For others, poor temper control is the form disinhibition takes. Such students are vulnerable to being led to carry out wrongful acts or setting themselves up for verbal or physical altercations.

It is appropriate to discuss the issue of compliance when covering the behaviors that directly impinge on classroom management. The lowest level of compliance is none. But be assured that students this noncompliant are more likely to be assigned to very restrictive settings (e.g., residential schools). Because the law protects children against inappropriate placement, it is possible that a very noncompliant student will first be given a chance in a general school program. Schools do not tolerate physically aggressive, noncompliant students for very long. Either the student improves quickly, or is suspended from school. Students sometimes cover up their noncompliance by pretending innocence or confusion. They are often argumentative in the classroom, even while being reasonably courteous (and exasperating). This can consume a lot of a teacher's attention, yet, the behavior may demonstrate some elements that the student is regaining control over his or her environment. Later, much more manipulation is observable in a more subtle form of noncompliance, for which teachers can be grateful because it represents progress. These gradations of behavior are difficult to interpret, because it is not always clear that these students understand what is expected or that they remember accurately. For example, one student was judged to be indifferent to a teacher's rule to return to the classroom immediately after using the bathroom. He was not really being belligerent, but was being distracted by whomever he met there. Another student pretended to be lost whenever he was discovered in a part of the school where his friends were. Several discoveries of that sort provide evidence of intent rather than confusion, but the distinction is not always so apparent.

As has been previously discussed, patients with frontal lobe injury often demonstrate difficulty with motivation. Such lack of motivation may be interpreted as a disorder of conduct, when, in reality, it may be organic in nature. In the early stages of recovery, motivation is moot. Patients are highly dependent on the nursing staff and become accustomed to having all choices made for them. This dependence may still exist for students who return to school with disability following a prolonged hospital stay. Moreover, impairment of memory and thought processes contributes to much perplexity and hampers achievement. Changes in physical dependence may improve motivation but mental work is still exhausting for the head-injured student, and the adjustment to school is difficult.

For some patients each act must be directed. Although they know how to dress and feed themselves, they do not do so until directed. Seriously impaired students may level off at such a state. They may demonstrate total lack of motivation, or having shown a desire to accomplish something, may lack the initiative to carry it out. This type of student may require cues to carry out even a highly structured activity.

Behavior management techniques have proven useful in helping students with head injuries develop self-control. To a large extent, loss of control is a function of the injury. Hyperphagia, disinhibition, perseveration, and silliness are all evidence of the loss of control. Structure is needed for the student with a head injury, and behavior management techniques are among the means of providing that structure. For example, one 15-year-old boy interrupted inappropriately, spoke out in class, and was generally disruptive. A token system was devised to provide the structure he needed to stay in control. When the desired behavior was made specific and the consequences tied to something he wanted (reinforcing), he managed to check himself and comply with the request for better classroom behavior. Another boy, 11 years old and wheelchair-bound, was extremely manipulative in trying to avoid physical therapy. Ultimately, the entire team had to be informed of the behavior and then united in consistent responses to that behavior. When several teachers have contact with a student, they must communicate frequently so that they can agree on procedures and respond consistently. Behavior management requires persistence and consistency. The behavior management principles remain the same:

- Ignore unwanted behavior; reinforce desired behavior; guard against reinforcing the very behavior that is unwanted.
- Conduct can also be managed by altering the environment. For some youngsters with head injury, large groups of people contribute to confusion and distraction. A structured environment is more easily maintained by small teacher-pupil ratios.
- A small class, in itself, is not necessarily structured. Close supervision is required and all activities must be goal directed.
- In general, there should not be large blocks of free time.

Insight

In the very early stages of recovery, there is little self-awareness. The metacognitive behavior of standing outside of oneself and examining oneself really is an advanced skill. We know that, developmentally, children demonstrate egocentric behavior until around the age of 8 or 9, and then gradually develop more sensitivity toward others as they relinquish this self-centered view. Much of the recovery from coma resembles passing through all the developmental periods from birth on. As recovery progresses, awareness develops and is a sign of progress.

When patients begin to feel self-conscious and resist going out, it is really a positive change — even while we acknowledge that they have a new problem. Overt fatigue and sadness mark this period, which often persists into the first year. Students may respond with irritability and impatience with themselves and others. Teachers are likely to observe this period of low self-esteem and irritability in returning head-injured students.

- To offset the student's fatigue, school personnel can provide rest periods or allow the student to attend only a partial day.
- To assist in the adjustment back into school during this period of low self-esteem, regular contact with the guidance counselor or psychologist is also advised.

A further stage of despair may develop for some students, even while they are still patients. Sometimes patients make suicidal threats, and indeed want to commit suicide when they face the loss of mobility, independence, personal attractiveness, and competence. Such despair affects the "A" student who now has trouble with school work that had been easy; the swimming champ who wanted to go to college on a sports scholarship (and could have) until the injury; the star football player on whom the whole team was counting to glorify their season; or the student with a long record of failure in school who now has even more trouble learning. Most of the suicidal statements are from adolescents, a population that has a high suicide rate without head injury; but younger children also express sadness and utter disappointment with themselves. The irony of this is that the ability to judge oneself and compare life now with then, and project possibilities into the future are all signs of progress and recovery. The severely damaged child lacks this awareness.

- Teachers must have sensitivity to the child who has recovered enough to be aware but still has not recovered enough for self-acceptance. This child returns to school with great self-doubt and hesitancy.
- Professionals know that any suicide threat has to be taken seriously. Even though it may be certain that the student who has sustained head injury could not organize him-

or herself well enough to carry out the threat, the family and the school staff need to be alerted to any suicidal indications.

• Counseling and other supportive services should be explored.

In contrast to the serious nature of suicide, teachers may observe some students who have trouble directing themselves toward a particular task and whose mood is quite euphoric. Occasionally, students giggle a little more than is expected, revealing a still present inability to exert control.

Only as students are confronted with the return to school and the community, do they gain true insight into their deficits. In the clinical setting of the rehabilitation unit, patients often deny the extent of their impairments. Whether caused by the severity of their impaired functioning or by a lack of insight, some students never recognize the full range of their deficits.

Physical Adaptations

A common residual motor deficit is weakness on one side of the body (hemiparesis). If this affects the dominant side, then writing skills will be considerably altered. This and other motoric deficits alter ambulation and mobility; still others can affect speech motor control. Technology and ingenuity have produced many sophisticated mechanical and electronic devices that provide mobility, self-care, communication, and independence.

Physical adaptations to the school environment are needed to enable the student's mobility and access to classes and educational materials. Schools must also adapt for any sensory deficits, such as visual impairment, and provide such aids as enlarged print and reduced visual stimuli, or proper positioning and lighting of materials. "Buddies" help students find their way around a building and lend physical support, such as carrying books or lunches. A buddy system can also provide badly needed social support and interaction. Allowance needs to be made for the head-injured students' reduced speed in navigating corridors during class changes. Generally, a few minutes advanced dismissal is sufficient.

Use of Computers

There is much controversy over the use of computers for cognitive rehabilitation. Although professionals find value in the computers' versatility in addressing specific therapy goals, generalization to everyday function has not been proven. As computers are becoming more commonplace in our homes, classrooms, and businesses, there is an intrinsic value in becoming computer-competent. Further, computer technology can provide the needed compensations for many deficits of the student with head injury.

Benefits of computers in cognitive therapy include: (1) children enjoy using computers and are usually motivated to interact with the tools in the early stages of their recovery, (2) the storage, along with delayed and immediate feedback options available in many software programs allow the student to compete against him- or herself in the remediation of skills, (3) the therapist has control over the amount and speed of stimuli presented and can alter stimulation as the student progresses, and (4) there is now so much software available that the therapist can address many deficit areas through the use of computers. All computer assisted instruction (CAI) should be monitored by the teacher or therapist. The computer should never replace the professional. As with other educational materials, the computer should be considered a tool.

When selecting software, the teacher or therapist must also exercise caution. Many software programs claim to address skills that, in reality, they do not. Teachers are encouraged to purchase software only after a demonstration of its use has convinced them of its applicability and usefulness for their student. Here too, teachers needs to consider the physical impairments and sensory deficits of their student when selecting software. (See Figure 7-1.)

Hardware is available to adapt computers for access by the physically disabled student. Adapted keyboards, enlarged visuals, voice input and output, and a wide variety of switches make computer use possible for anyone who is cognitively able.

Students in Persistent Coma

Jennett and Plum (1985) define the vegetative state as: "some never regain recognizable mental function . . . have periods of

	NONSPEAKING	LIMITED ACCESS METHODS	VISUAL DEFICITS	HEARING IMPAIRED	ATTENTION DEFICITS	UNMOTIVATED	SLOW RESPONSE TIME	IMPULSIVE RESPONDING	MEMORY DEFICITS
AUDITORY FEEDBACK	✔		✔		✔	✔			✔
ADJUSTABLE VOLUME	✔		✔	✔					
LARGE SCREEN PRINT			✔						
SIMPLE GRAPHICS			✔		✔				
ADJUSTABLE PRESENTATION SPEED		✔	✔	✔	✔	✔		✔	✔
ADJUSTABLE RESPONSE TIME		✔	✔		✔	✔	✔	✔	✔
IMMEDIATE FEEDBACK	✔				✔	✔	✔	✔	✔
TRACKING OF RESPONSES							✔		✔
STORAGE OF PARTIAL DATA						✔			✔
REPETITION PROVIDED	✔				✔	✔		✔	✔	✔
VARIABLE INSTRUCTION LEVELS						✔			
VARIABLE ENTRY LEVELS						✔			
REDUCED KEY RESPONSES		✔					✔		
ATTRACTIVE GRAPHICS					✔	✔			
IMPORTANT DATA HIGHLIGHTED			✔		✔			✔	✔

Figure 7-1. Software selection criteria for individuals with cognitive, sensory, or psychomotor deficits. From *The Handbook of Assistive Technology* by G. Church and S. Glennen, 1992, San Diego: Singular Publishing Group, Inc. Copyright 1992 by Church and Glennen. Reprinted by permission.

wakefulness when their eyes are open and move, their responsiveness is limited to primitive postural and reflex movements of limbs and never speak." The terminology used to describe these unfortunate victims of severe traumatic head injury varies from persistent vegetative state, to prolonged coma, to post comatose unawareness (Sazbon & Groswasser, 1991). Medical and rehabilitation professionals struggle not only with its description, but also with its treatment and prognostic indicators.

Using both neurological and electrophysiological studies of patients in prolonged coma, researchers have begun to develop treatment protocols. Some propose the use of deep brain stimulation for use with a portion of these patients (Tsubokawa et al., 1990). Others support the use of coma arousal procedures (Mitchell, Bradley, Welch, & Britton, 1990). Although the use of coma stimulation and arousal therapy is fairly widespread in acute trauma care and rehabilitation, its effectiveness has not always been supported in research (Pierce et al., 1990). Many social, ethical, economic, and judicial questions emerge from the treatment available for these unfortunate patients.

The child or adolescent who remains in a state of generalized response (Ranchos Los Amigos level II) is still eligible for educational services. One provision of the law which provides education for all children is its "zero reject" component. Cases involving children in persistent coma are frequently in litigation or due process hearings. Consider the family of a previously normal youngster who now remains in a state of apparent unawareness. Knowing that this child previously had awareness, families often cling to the notion that the child is perceiving more than the child can communicate. On the other hand, the school system sees a student who, after months or years of therapy, has made no measurable progress. This moral and ethical controversy has recently been decided in favor of provision of services, regardless of measurable outcome. This stems, in part, from research in developmental psychology that maintains that if a level of sensory stimulation is not maintained, there appears to a deterioration in information processing mechanisms.

This student, as does any other severely and profoundly handicapped youngster, presents a challenge to the professionals who work with him or her. They must be tolerant of repetition, persistent in their search for new ideas, and content to accept little or no change. Because responses to stimulation are usually qualitative rather than quantitative, it is important to keep ongoing records of observations when working with these students. Graphing data can identify optimal sensory modalities, preferred times of day, preferred therapists, or favored activities.

Although sensory stimulation is recommended for these students, its duration and intensity needs to be monitored. One school, in an effort to do everything they could, placed a student in almost continual sensory stimulation. He went to music class, sat in a busy cafeteria at lunchtime, engaged in numerous therapies, and was provided with periods of one-to-one sensory stimulation. After monitoring his responses, the staff noted heightened agitation and sweating. When they modified his program for a balance of high- and low-stimulation environments, the student's quality of responses improved. In designing a program for these students, professionals must consider not only what services to provide, but also how to balance the students' activities to their specific needs in order to enhance optimal response to their environment.

Sensory stimulation programs can become monotonous for the staff members that have to carry them out. The Kennedy Krieger Institute Department of Occupational Therapy uses a checklist of activities from which the reader may draw some ideas. The actual instrument includes areas to record the response, date, time, and therapist's name. The list of activities has been extracted here. (See Figure 7-2.)

SUMMARY

The student returning to school following head injury can benefit from many of the same strategies and techniques employed with other student populations by skilled teachers. The education professional needs to be sensitive to the cognitive, motoric, and psychosocial profile of this type of student, and knowledgeable as to both the student's specific needs and the expected rate and course of further recovery. It is a particular challenge to work with the families of these students throughout this lengthy recovery period. The intervention of a number of professionals within the school setting may be required, with communication and team planning paramount to smooth reintegration and remediation.

Kennedy Krieger Institute
Department of Occupational Therapy
Sensory Stimulation Checklist

Visual
Lights
    overhead
    sunlight
    flashlight
    candle
    Lite Brite
Mirror
Magnifying Glass
    with lights
    without lights
Bubbles
Mobiles
Animals
Wind Up Toy
Crepe Paper on Stick
Video Tape of Patient
_____
_____
_____

Olfactory
Candles that Smell
flowers
Mouth Wash
Perfume/After Shave
    familiar
Shaving Cream
Spices and Seasonings
Pleasant
    banana
    coffee
    cloves
    cinnamon
    ginger
    nutmeg
    orange
    peppermint
    strawberry
    vanilla
    wintergreen
Unpleasant
    alcohol
    chili powder
    garlic
    onion
    vinegar
_____
_____
_____

Figure 7-2. Kennedy Krieger Institute Occupational Therapy Sensory Stimulation Checklist.

Figure 7-2. (continued)

Movement
Bouncing on Ball
Rocking
    in chair
    on board
    over ball
Swinging
    linear
    angular
Riding in Wagon
    fast
    swervy

_____
_____
_____

Auditory
Voices
    children's
    adult (m/f)
    familiar
    unfamiliar
Music
    records
    radio
    fast
    slow
Musical Instruments
    xylophone
    whistle
    bells
    wood block
    cymbals
    tambourine
    organ
    piano
    maraca
    clapping
    snapping

Gustatory
**Check with OT as to precautions.
End tastes with toothette or
swab.**
Pleasant
    bananas
    orange
    ice cream
    spices
    extracts
    jelly
    marshmallow
    peanut butter
    toothette

_____

Unpleasant
    lemon
    pepper
    vinegar
    soy sauce
    worcestershire sauce
    salad dressing

_____
_____
_____

Figure 7-2. (continued)

Auditory (continued)
Music Boxes
Bicycle Horn
Traffic Noises
See-and-Say
Happy Apple
Timer
Vibrator
Jangling keys

Tactile
Cold
   ice
   snow
   foods
Warm
   bath
   hair dryer
   heating pad
   foods
   Ben Gay

Tactile (continued)
Soft Textures
   cotton
   bubble bath
   fabric
   flannel
   fur
   foam
   feathers
   jello
   lotion
   rabbit
   towel
   wet oatmeal
Rough Textures
   brush
   carpet squares
   dry oatmeal
   macaroni
   rice
   sand
Smooth Texture
   clay
   finger paints
   jello
   lotion
   cooked noodles
   pudding
Touch
   firm
   light
   tickling
Vibration
   cold
   soft cloth
   towel

Notion Used:
  + **response noted**
  - **no response noted**

Chapter **8**

Summary and Issues

Even in implementing the optimal reintegration plan, with school staff and administrators given some inservice training regarding head trauma, many questions and problems are not anticipated. In all fairness to educational professionals, rehabilitation therapists have emphasized the unique outcomes and impairments in children and adolescents who have sustained head trauma and, in essence, told them, as we have the parents of the students, to take each day as it comes with a watchful eye for some common problems. In addition, educational professionals have been mandated to serve all youngsters, and are often reluctant to admit that they are not prepared for every eventuality. Problems reported after school reentry are usually voiced as a failure of the student to comply with or benefit from the educational program, rather than problems the staff might have had in understanding the student.

The following questions are ones that should be discussed during the school reentry process whether they are initiated by the teachers or the rehabilitation professionals:

Q: Is it harmful or advisable to refer to the student's accident? Will it revive bad memories or stigmatize the student in the eyes of peers?

A: It is inevitable that many questions will be asked of the student on return to school. Children and adolescents are curious and concerned. It is usually helpful to prepare classmates before the student's return. This avoids a barrage of questions on the first day. The question of the student's wishes regarding discussion of the accident should be posed prior to return to school and the student's wishes on this matter conveyed to school personnel.

A head-injured student might respond to questions posed in the school setting with tearfulness or giggling. This is more likely to be the manifestation of emotional lability than the restoration of deep feeling about his or her experience.

Q: How are head-injured students affected by noise and high levels of stimulation?

A: Because the brain controls all of our functions, it is logical to assume that head trauma could result in sensory disturbance. Frequently students who have sustained head trauma are acutely aware of noise, movement, and smell. Others are highly distracted by visual stimulation or movement. Corridors and cafeterias can be especially difficult for these reasons.

There is also a period when some individuals experience "internal noise." This is an aggravation caused by increased distractibility, unclear thinking, associative reasoning, poor memory, and impulsivity. The student can become aggravated and confused by not only his or her environment, but also by internal malfunction of the damaged brain.

Q: Can students who have experienced head trauma participate in physical education?

A: Most physicians recommend that during the first year following the injury the student refrain from contact sports or any other activities with a high risk for additional head trauma. This issue should be reevaluated at medical follow-up appointments. This does not preclude the student from participating in physical education, but may require some adaptations to the physical education program or consultations with a physical therapist by the physical education teacher.

Q: Is it alright for head-injured students to take drivers' education classes?

A: Allowing students to participate in drivers' education classes leads them to anticipate driving after they have passed the written and road tests, whereas the actual ability to do so will depend on their motor coordination, vision, reaction time, and judgment. These later qualifications may be lacking in the first few years following head trauma. As passing the test will give students the means to put strong pressure on their parents to allow car use (often against their better judgment), it is recommended that drivers' education classes be deferred. The best approach to the issue of driving after sustaining head trauma is to seek a driving evaluation by rehabilitation professionals specializing in this area. These evaluators are especially attuned to the particular deficits following head trauma that may interfere with safe operation of a motor vehicle.

Q: Should students with head injury wear helmets?

A: Helmets are rarely prescribed at discharge from the rehabilitation program. Wearing a helmet stigmatizes youngsters, and it is usually unnecessary during school activities. If the student's balance remains unstable, he or she can be taught how to fall with protective reactions.

Sometimes school administrators worry about liability, but if the physical therapist and the physician did not prescribe a helmet, then administrators should relax.

Promoting the use of a helmet for cycling, skating, and skate boarding is highly recommended for all students.

Q: Is this student likely to have seizures, and, if so, what should I do?

A: Seizures are common in some children and adolescents who have experienced head trauma, depending on the severity of the injury. Teachers should be informed by the family or hospital personnel if a student has had seizures, a description of episodes, what is being done to manage seizures, and what procedures should be followed when they occur. This information might be best managed by the school nurse, who can advise the staff how to respond.

Q: What supervision is needed during a fire drill?

A: If the student is in the classroom, no extra supervision is required. If the student is out of the classroom (e.g., going to therapy or the health room), someone should be responsible for finding and escorting him or her from the building.

Q: Can head-injured students participate in home economics and industrial arts classes?

A: Safety in cooking, sewing, and operation of power machinery is an issue for many students who have sustained head trauma. Their inclusion in these classes will depend on fine motor control, reaction time, memory, and judgment. The instructor or an occupational therapist may help assess the advisability of a particular student attending these classes.

Q: What expectations are there regarding the student's social readjustment in the school setting?

A: The student usually receives a great deal of emotional and social support from his or her previous peer group on initial return to school. Even well-meaning and supportive friends typically drift away as they begin to experience the differences in the student who has sustained head trauma. Cognitive, psychosocial, and motoric impairments all affect how the student can resume interaction with his or her friends. It is not unusual for teachers and parents to notice that the student with head trauma develops a new peer group, or experiences social isolation.

Some general practices may be helpful in answering questions not raised here:

- Try to keep the demands on students with head injury consistent with what is expected of others, especially socially.
- When behavior is erratic or negative behaviors persist, look for a reason related to the injury (memory, poor orientation, hypersensitivity, and so forth); supply enough structure to correct the situation rather than assume this student is unmotivated, recalcitrant, or stupid.

- Confront behavior in a nonjudgmental, matter-of-fact manner, pointing out what is appropriate or inappropriate and suggesting an alternative behavior.
- There is no need to be reticent about head trauma; open discussion with all students may promote more understanding among others and less embarrassment for the injured. Sometimes patients fear that head trauma will be interpreted as craziness or retardation. Patients at the Kennedy Krieger Institute are taught to acknowledge their injuries and to identify some of the problems they are experiencing.
- Ask for as much information as possible from the family, hospital, social worker, or anyone working professionally with this individual. Ask what to expect, what current problems people recognize, what is now different as a result of the injury, how severe the injury was, what therapy needs still exist, and what is needed for adaptation back into the school setting. Even though teachers are not responsible for all facets of recovery, having a lot of information helps fill in the global picture of the head-injured student.
- Stay in touch with therapists and family members. Ask what carryover is needed in the classroom. Work as a team; communication between school and home is more important than ever during reintegration.

PROBLEMS FROM THE FAMILY'S POINT OF VIEW

By the time head-injured students return to school, parents have been through a lot. In those instances where children remain very severely damaged, very deep grief is felt over the loss of normal children, and perhaps parents also harbor some amount of ambivalence about whether it would have been better after all if their child had died. There is no closure for the grief, because there is still a living child. One parent, discussing his predicament as a widowed father trying to manage a very difficult teenaged daughter, said eloquently, "I used to pray to God to spare my daughter's life. God answered my prayers but I didn't know what I was going to get. Now, I've got to make the best of things." Families need a lot of support from many sources, but especially they need the cooperation and understanding of their child's teachers.

In an informal questionnaire which explored the problems that families encountered in resuming their child's school participation, parents experienced the following difficulties to some extent:

- Lack of teacher understanding;
- Uncooperative and insensitive mainstream teachers;
- Loss of friends for child, particularly during the transition to a new school or new classes; social isolation; rare invitations by friends;
- Parental isolation (e.g., one mother was no longer asked to volunteer at school; another felt avoided by parents of her child's friends);
- Parental strain from working with children on homework;
- Class placement sometimes thought to be inappropriate.

All emphasized the importance of and their gratitude for support from teachers.

PROBLEMS FROM THE PROFESSIONAL'S POINT OF VIEW

The Maryland Head Injury Foundation reports that families experience much frustration in finding needed services in the community, and in obtaining the funding resources needed to secure help. Further problems may arise in the coordination of services among several agencies, when a comprehensive service is not available.

Shorter hospital admissions followed by long periods of outpatient rehabilitation are a current trend. The primary reason for the shorter hospitalization is the intense economic pressure to curtail hospital costs. Patients are generally discharged when a physician determines that they are medically stable, and when a multidisciplinary team determines that the family can manage an outpatient program. This sort of rationale places a heavy burden on outpatient facilities and school systems that are sometimes ill-equipped to handle the head-injured patient.

Although inpatient rehabilitation programs offer intensive therapy to prepare the child to return home and reenter school, educational systems cannot count on these facilities to provide information and ongoing communication. The responsibility is mutual, and if there is no outreach from the rehabilitation professionals, the school should take the initiative to develop a relationship.

Related services provided under the federal mandates for free and appropriate education for all children are important resources for rehabilitation patients. Physical, occupational, speech, and counseling therapies are provided to eligible students as a part of their comprehensive curriculum. Otherwise, many communities lack these important services, and, thus, the school system is the sole provider of therapeutic needs for educational reintegration. In addition, special education provides an interdisciplinary framework for a student to be supported, with therapists, teachers, family, and ancillary staff cooperating in day-to-day program management. Centralized treatment should continue, providing for frequent reassessment as the student's clinical and educational needs change. One member of the educational team should be assigned as case manager. This job includes being the liaison between the school and the hospital or rehabilitation program when it is necessary to cooperate on common goals. The case manager coordinates ongoing services throughout the community for the child and family.

Because of the need for interdisciplinary cooperation, it is beneficial to have needed services centralized in a single community agency. If the school system does not assume this function, then a community agency with as many services as possible is recommended. This concentration of services prevents unnecessary and difficult transportation, duplication of services, and inconsistent management due to differences in therapeutic approach. If division of services is unavoidable, the case manager's coordination of services is especially important in the long-term treatment of a student with persistent deficits resulting from head injury. A sudden change in a particular deficit may influence management in other areas. Further, posttraumatic treatment of these deficits is not standard in any discipline. Therapists of various disciplines may operate according to theoretical formulations that are in pronounced disagreement to the strategies of other workers. If disagreements among therapists hamper a student's progress, the team must meet to reassess the patient's needs and arrive at a consensus about further therapeutic strategies. Teachers should play a primary role in this, as the goal of the related services is to increase independence and proficiency in the educational setting; the teacher's observations of the student's classroom behavior and achievement should guide the development of treatment approaches.

Availability of school-delivered services, including classroom instruction, is very uneven. Although the mandate of the law is clear, systems vary in ability to provide. Sometimes, funded positions remain unfilled for lack of available therapists.

Availability of educational professionals trained in the education and treatment of students who have sustained head trauma cannot be assumed. Some states, such as Maryland, have made an effort to train special education administrators regarding the sequelae of head trauma, but, still, many of the teachers and support staff who will work with these youngsters have not had training. Several colleges and universities now mention this population in introductory special education courses, and the Johns Hopkins University in Baltimore, Maryland, has begun to offer a minicourse for teaching professionals and related service providers.

Availability of classroom instruction depends on the coincidence of the injury with the school year. The critical period of reentry for a child injured in the spring generally falls in the summer, a bleak time to find services and schooling. In these cases, the sorely needed structure, routine, instruction, and opportunities for socialization have to be put on hold until September, while immediate needs for therapy can be sought from among various private sector programs. Appropriate day camp programs are almost nonexistent. Most of the day camp or summer school options available are designed for children who are developmentally delayed, or for remediation in subjects a general-population student has recently failed. Although remediation classes might appear to meet the needs of some students who are impaired, they are often too intensive and too brief for students who have sustained head injury.

PSYCHIATRIC CLASSIFICATION

The classification of psychiatric disorders is currently under revision, with emphasis on defining diagnostic criteria supported by carefully conducted clinical research studies. The Diagnostic and Statistical Manuals III and III-R published in 1980 and 1987 attempted to group psychologic or behavioral abnormalities associated with transient or permanent brain dysfunction into a section on organic mental disorders. Categories of organic mental disorders include those diagnoses that are most frequently applied to patients with head injury when a psychiatric diagnosis is necessary. These disorders include delirium, dementia, amnestic syndrome, organic delusional syndrome, organic mood syndrome, and organic personality syndrome.

The prevailing opinion is that the organic/nonorganic distinction in psychiatry is obsolete. The term organic has implied a biologic or physiologic basis for a disorder, in contrast to the term nonorganic, which has implied a nonbiologic or nonpsychologic basis for the disorder. Biologic and physiologic contributions are now being defined for most psychiatric disorders, including anxiety and depression.

Because of these developments, a conceptual reorganization of the organic mental disorders is being proposed for the DSM-IV manual expected in 1993. The proposed classification would group the three diagnoses of delirium, dementia, and amnestic disorder into a category of Cognitive Impairment Disorders, because cognitive impairment is the predominant feature of all three. An alternative would be to call the group Delirium, Dementia, Amnestic Disorder. The other organic mental disorders would be placed in the sections with which they share fundamental features and the term "organic" would be replaced by the term "secondary." In addition, the medical condition would be included as part of the name (Task Force on DSM-IV, 1991). For example, a depressive disorder after head injury would be called "Secondary Mood Disorder Due to Severe Closed Head Injury" in the proposed new classification. This proposal appears to provide a more precise descriptive terminology for those psychiatric disorders that occur as a result of head injury.

A lack of common terminology by the disciplines involved in the study and treatment of cognitive and psychiatric disorders may confound diagnosis and interdisciplinary communication. Psychiatrists, speech-language pathologists, clinical psychologists, behavioral psychologists, social workers, and educators have each developed a respective terminology, system of diagnosis, and treatment modalities for their clients. Each group may use a different term to describe a certain ailment or the same term to describe different ailments. Many speech-language pathologists and occupational therapists utilize the Rancho Los Amigos Scale in their therapeutic work. (See Appendix C.) However, this scale does not use medical terms such as "coma" or "posttraumatic amnesia," nor does it describe psychiatric features such as hallucinations or sleep/wake disturbances. Perhaps, as a result, this scale is not used in medical and psychiatric research studies.

It is worthwhile for members of the rehabilitation interdisciplinary team to hold periodic discussions about terminology and to strive for consensus about the meanings of commonly used terms such as agitation, attention, dysphagia, and posttraumatic amnesia. Such an agreement about meaning enables team members to communicate efficiently in clinical care and in conducting research and service projects.

Appendix **A**

GLASGOW COMA SCALE

EYE OPENING
    Spontaneous   E4
    To Speech   3
    To Pain   2
    Nil   1
BEST MOTOR RESPONSE
    Obeys   M6
    Localizes   5
    Withdraws   4
    Abnormal flexion   3
    Extensor response   2
    Nil   1
VERBAL RESPONSE
    Oriented   V5
    Confused conversation   4
    Inappropriate words   3
    Incomprehensible sounds   2
    Nil   1

COMA SCORE (E+M+V) = 3 to 15

From *Management of head injuries* by B. Jennett and G. Teasdale, 1981, Philadelphia: F.A. Davis. Copyright 1981 by Jennett and Teasdale. Reprinted by permission.

Appendix **B**

CHILDREN'S ORIENTATION AND AMNESIA TEST (COAT)

Name _____Date of Test _____
Age _____ Sex M F   Day of the Week S M T W T F S
Date of Birth _____   Time   AM   PM
Diagnosis _____Date of Injury_____

INSTRUCTIONS FOR EXAMINER: Begin by introducing
yourself by name (e.g., "Dr. _____") and ask the child
to be sure to remember your name. Points for correct responses
(shown in parentheses after each question) are scored and en-
tered in the columns on the extreme right side of the test form.
Enter the total points accrued for the items in the lower right
corner of the test form. Children ages 3 to 7 are administered
only the General Orientation and Memory sections of the test.
The entire test is administered to children ages 8 to 15.

General Orientation   Points:
  1. What is your name? first (2) _____
     last (3) _____   (5)_____
  2. How old are you? (3) _____
     When is your birthday? month (1) _____
     day (1) _____   (5)_____
  3. Where do you live? city (3) _____
     state (2) _____ (5)_____
  4. What is your father's name? (5) _____
     What is your mother's name? (5) _____ (10)_____

5. What school do you go to? (3) _____
   What grade are you in? (2) _____ (5)_____
6. Where are you now? (5)_____ (5)_____
   (May rephrase question: Are you at home now? Are
   you in the hospital? If rephrased, child must
   correctly answer both questions to receive
   credit.)
7. Is it daytime or nighttime? (5) _____ (5)_____
                    General Orientation Total   _____

Temporal Orientation
8. What time is it now? (5) _____(5)_____
   (correct = 5; 1/2 hr. off = 4; 1 hr. off = 3;
   greater than 1 hr. off = 2; 2 hrs. off = 1)
9. What day of the week is it? (5) _____ (5)_____
   (correct = 5; 1 off = 4; 2 off = 3; 3 off = 2;
   4 off = 1)
10. What day of the month is it? (5) _____ (5)_____
    (correct = 5; 1 off = 4; 2 off = 3; 3 off = 2;
    4 off = 1)
11. What is the month? (10) _____ (10)_____
    (correct = 10; 1 off = 7; 2 off = 4; 3 off = 1)
12. What is the year? (15) _____ (15)_____
    (correct = 15; 1 off = 10; 2 off = 5; 3 off = 1)
                    Temporal Orientation Total   _____

Memory
13. Say these numbers after me in the same order. (Discontin-
    ue when the child fails both series of digits at any length.
    Score2 points if both digit series are correctly repeated; score
    1 point if only 1 is correct.)

3	5_____	35296	81493 _____		
58	42_____	539418	724856 _____		
643	926_____	8129365	4739128 _____	(14) ___	
7216	3279_____				

14. How many fingers am I holding up?
    2 fingers (2) _____   3 fingers (3) _____
    10 fingers (5) _____   (10) _____
15. Who is on Sesame Street? (10) _____ (10)_____
    (can substitute other major television show)

16. What is my name? (10) _____   (10) _____

                     Memory Total   _____
                     OVERALL TOTAL   _____
NOTE: (Question 5, General Orientation)

If a child age 3 to 6 correctly states that he or she does not attend school, give full credit. For children enrolled in pre-school, credit is given for stating the teacher's name in lieu of stating the grade.

_____

From "The Children's Orientation and Amnesia Test: Relationship to severity of acute head injury and to recovery of memory" by L. Ewing-Cobbs, H.S. Levin, J.M. Fletcher, M.E. Miner, and H.M. Eisenberg. *Neurosurgery*, *27*(5), p. 684, (1990). Reprinted by permission.

Appendix C

RANCHO LOS AMIGOS
LEVELS OF COGNITIVE FUNCTIONING

I. **No Response:** Patient appears to be in a deep sleep and is completely unresponsive to any stimuli.

II. **Generalized Response:** Patient reacts inconsistently and nonpurposefully to stimuli in a nonspecific manner. Responses are limited and often the same, regardless of stimulus presented. Responses may be physiological changes, gross body movements, and/or vocalization.

III. **Localized Response:** Patient reacts specifically, but inconsistently, to stimuli. Responses are directly related to the type of stimulus presented. May follow simple commands such as, "Close your eyes" or "Squeeze my hand" in an inconsistent, delayed manner.

IV. **Confused-Agitated:** Behavior is bizarre and nonpurposeful relative to immediate environment. Does not discriminate among persons or objects, is unable to cooperate directly with treatment efforts, verbalizations are frequently incoherent and/or inappropriate to the environment, confabulation may be present. Gross attention to environment is very short, and selective attention is often nonexistent. Patient lacks short-term recall.

V. **Confused, Inappropriate, Nonagitated:** Patient is able to respond to simple commands fairly consistently. However, with increased complexity of commands, or lack of any external structure, responses are nonpurposeful, random, or fragmented. Has gross attention to the environment, but is highly distractible, and lacks ability to focus attention on a specific task; with structure, may be able to converse on a social/automatic level for short periods of time; verbalization is often inappropriate and confabulatory; memory is severely impaired; often shows inappropriate use of subjects; may perform previously learned tasks with structure, but is unable to learn new information.

VI.   **Confused-Appropriate:** Patient shows goal-directed behavior, but is dependent on external input for direction; follows simple directions consistently and shows carry-over for relearned tasks with little or no carry-over for new tasks; responses may be incorrect due to memory problems, but appropriate to the situation; past memories show more depth and detail than recent memory.

VII.   **Automatic-Appropriate:** Patient appears appropriate and oriented within hospital and home settings, goes through daily routine automatically, but is frequently robot-like, with minimal-to-absent confusion; has shallow recall of activities; shows carry-over for new learning, but at a decreased rate; with structure, is able to initiate social or recreational activities; judgment remains impaired.

VIII. **Purposeful and Appropriate:** Patient is able to recall and integrate past and recent events, and is aware of and responsive to the environment; shows carry-over for new learning and needs no supervision once activities are learned; may continue to show a decreased ability, relative to premorbid abilities in language, abstract reasoning, tolerance for stress and judgment in emergencies or unusual circumstances.

From "Language disorders in head trauma" by Chris Hagen in *Handbook of speech and language disorders*, edited by Janis M. Costello and Audrey L. Holland, 1986, San Diego: College-Hill Press. Reprinted by permission.

References

Adamovich, B.B., & Henderson, J.A. (1990). Treatment of communication deficits resulting from closed head injury. In L. LaPoint (Ed.). *Aphasia and related neurogenic language disorders.* New York: Thieme Medical Publishers, Inc.

American Psychiatric Association. (1987). *Diagnostic and statistical manual of mental disorders* (3rd ed. rev.). Washington, DC: Author.

American Psychiatric Association. (1991). *DSM-IV options book: Work in progress.* Washington, DC: Author.

Barnard, P., Dill, H., Eldredge, P., Held, J.M., Judd, D.L.M., & Nalette, E. (1984). Reduction of hypertonicity by early casting in a comatose head-injured individual. *Physical Therapy, 64,* 1540-1542.

Bender, L. (1938). *A visual motor gestalt test and its clinical use.* New York: American Orthopsychiatric Association.

Berrol, S. (1990). Issues in cognitive rehabilitation. *Archives of Neurology, 47,* 219-220.

Beukelman, D.R., Yorkston, K., & Dowden, P. (1985). *Communication augmentation: A casebook of clinical management.* San Diego: College-Hill Press.

Blosser, J.L., & DePompei, R. (1989). The head-injured student returns to school: Recognizing and treating deficits. *Topics in Language Disorders, 9*(2), 67-77.

Brink, J.D., Garrett, A.L., Hale, W.R., Woo-Sam, J., & Nickel, V.L. (1970). Recovery of motor and intellectual function in children sustaining severe head injuries. *Developmental Medicine and Child Neurology, 12,* 565-571.

Brink, J.D., Imbus, C., & Woo-Sam, J. (1980). Physical recovery after closed head trauma in children and adolescents. *Journal of Pediatrics, 97,* 721-727.

Brooks, N. (1991). The effectiveness of post-acute rehabilitation [Editorial]. *Brain Injury, 5,* 103-109.

Brown, G., Chadwick, D., Shaffer, D., Rutter, M., & Traub, M. (1981). A prospective study of children with head injuries: III. Psychiatric sequelae. *Psychological Medicine, 11*(1), 63-78.

Bruce, D.A. (1983). Management of cerebral edema. *Pediatrics in Review, 4,* 217-224.

Bruce, D.A. (1990). Head injuries in the pediatric population. *Current Problems in Pediatrics, 20*(2), 63-107.

Bruce, D.A., Raphaely, R.C., Goldberg, A.I., Zimmerman, R.A.,Bilaniuk, L.T., Schut, L., & Kuhl, D.E. (1979). Pathophysiology, treatment and outcome following severe head injury in children. *Child's Brain, 5,* 174-191.

Chadwick, O., Rutter, M., Brown, G., Shaffer, D., & Traub, M. (1981). A prospective study of children with head injuries: 2. Cognitive sequelae. *Psychological Medicine, 11*(1), 49-61.

Chelune, G.J., & Baer, R.A. (1986). Developmental norms for the Wisconsin Card Sorting Test. *Journal of Clinical and Experimental Neuropsychology, 8,* 219-228.

Church, G., & Glennen, S. (1992). *The handbook of assistive technology.* San Diego: Singular Publishing Group, Inc.

Clark, R.G. (1975). *Manter and Gatz's Essentials of clinical neuroanatomy and neurophysiology.* Philadelphia: F.A. Davis.

Cope, D.N., Cole, J.R., Hall, K.M., & Barkan, H. (1991a). Brain injury: Analysis of outcome in a post-acute rehabilitation system. Part 1: General analysis. *Brain Injury, 5,* 111-125.

Cope, D.N., Cole, J.R., Hall, K.M., & Barkan, H. (1991b). Brain injury: Analysis of outcome in a post-acute rehabilitation system. Part 2: Subanalyses. *Brain Injury, 5,* 127-139.

Crosby, E.C., Humphrey, T., & Lauer, E.W. (1962). *Correlative anatomy of the nervous system.* New York: The Macmillan Co.

Denckla, M.B. (1989). Executive function, the overlap zone between attention deficit hyperactivity disorder and learning disabilities. *International Pediatrics, 4,* 155-160.

Dennis, M. (1991). Frontal lobe function in childhood and adolescence: A heuristic for assessing attention, regulation, executive control and the intentional states important for social discourse. *Developmental Neuropsychology, 7*(11), 327-358.

Di Scala, C., Osberg, J.S., Gans, B.M., Chin, L.J., & Grant, C.C. (1991). Children with traumatic head injury: Morbidity and postacute treatment. *Archives of Physical Medicine and Rehabilitation, 72,* 662-666.

Emick-Herring, B., & Wood, P. (1990). A team approach to neurologically based swallowing disorders. *Rehabilitation Nursing, 15,* 126-132.

Ewert, J., Levin, H.S., Watson, M.G., & Kalisky, Z. (1989). Procedural memory during posttraumatic amnesia in survivors of severe closed head injury. Implications for rehabilitation. *Archives of Neurology, 46,* 911-916.

Ewing-Cobbs, L., Levin, H.S., Fletcher, J.M., Miner, M.M., & Eisenberg, H.M. (1990). The Children's Orientation and Amnesia Test: Relationship to severity of acute head injury and to recovery of memory. *Neurosurgery, 27*(5), 683-691.

Gaidolfi, E., & Vignolo, L.A. (1980). Closed head injuries of school-age children: Neuropsychological sequelae in early adulthood. *Italian Journal of Neurological Sciences, 1,* 65-73.

Gasquoine, P.G. (1991). Learning in post-traumatic amnesia following extremely severe closed head injury. *Brain Injury, 5,* 169-175.

Gentry, L.R., Godersky, J.C., & Thompson, B. (1988). MR imaging of head trauma: Review of the distribution and radiopathologic features of traumatic lesions. *American Journal of Neuroradiology, 150,* 663-672.

Gerring, J.P., & McCarthy, L.P. (1988). *The psychiatry of handicapped children and adolescents: Managing emotional and behavioral problems*. Boston: Little, Brown and Company.

Gilchrist, E., & Wilkinson, M. (1979). Some factors determining prognosis in young people with severe head injuries. *Archives of Neurology, 36*, 355-359.

Goldstein, F.G., & Levin, H.S. (1985). Intellectual and academic outcome following closed head injury in children and adolescents: Research strategies and empirical findings. *Developmental Neuropsychology, 1*(3), 195-214.

Greenberg, L. (1988). *The Minnesota Computerized Assessment*. Minneapolis: University of Minnesota Press.

Gronwall, D., & Sampson, H. (1974). *Psychological effects of concussion*. Auckland, New Zealand: Auckland University Press.

Guthkelch, A.N. (1979). Posttraumatic amnesia, post-concussional symptoms and accident. *Acta Neurochirurgica* (Suppl. 28), 120-123.

Hagen, C. (1986). Language disorders in head trauma. In J.M. Costello & A.L. Holland (Eds.), *Handbook of speech and language disorders*. San Diego: College-Hill Press.

Hall, K., Cope, N., & Rappaport, M. (1985). Glasgow Outcome Scale and Disability Rating Scale: Comparative usefulness in following recovery in traumatic head injury. *Archives of Physical Medicine and Rehabilitation, 66*, 35-37.

Healy, G.B. (1982). Hearing loss and vertigo secondary to head injury. *New England Journal of Medicine, 306*, 1029-1031.

Heaton, R.T. (1981). *Wisconsin Card Sorting Test manual*. Odessa, FL: Psychological Assessment Resources.

Herrington, R.N. (1969). The personality in temporal lobe epilepsy. In R.N. Herrington (Ed.). *British Journal of Psychiatry* (Special Publication No. 4). Ashford, Kent, England: Headley Brothers.

Hillbom, E. (1960). After-effects of brain injuries. *Acta Psychiatrica et Neurologica Scandinavica, 35*(Suppl. 142), 1-195.

Jennett, B., & Plum, F. (1985). Persistent vegetative state. *Archives of Neurology, 42*, 1405-1407.

Jennett, B., Snoek, J., Bond, M.R., & Brooks, N. (1981). Disability after severe head injury: Observations on the use of the Glasgow Outcome Scale. *Journal of Neurology, Neurosurgery and Psychiatry, 44*, 285-293.

Jennett, B., & Teasdale, G. (1981). *Management of head injuries*. Philadelphia: F.A. Davis.

Johnston, M.V., & Lewis, F.D. (1991). Outcomes of community re-entry programmes for brain injury survivors. Part 1: Independent living and productive activities. *Brain Injury, 5*, 141-154.

Kelly, A.B., Zimmerman, R.D., Snow, R.B., Gandy, S.E., Heier, L.A., & Deck, M.D.F. (1988). Head trauma: Comparison of MR and CT-Experience in 100 patients. *American Journal of Neurology, 9*, 699-708.

Knights, R.M., Ivan, L.P., Ventureyra, E.C.G., Bentivoglio, C., Stoddart, C., Winogron, W., & Bawden, H.N. (1991). The effects of head injury in children on neuropsychological and behavioral functioning. *Brain Injury, 5*, 339-351.

Kolb, B., & Whishaw, I.D. (1980). *Fundamentals of human neuropsychology*. San Francisco: W.H. Freeman and Co.

Kraus, J.F., Fife, D., & Conroy, C. (1987). Pediatric brain injuries: The nature, clinical course and early outcomes in a defined United States' population. *Pediatrics, 79*, 501-507.

Kriel, R.L., Krach, L.E., & Panser, L.A. (1989). Closed head injury: Comparison of children younger and older than 6 years of age. *Pediatric Neurology,* *5,* 296-300.

Kriel, R.L., Krach, L.E., & Sheehan, M. (1988). Pediatric closed head injury: Outcome following prolonged unconsciousness. *Archives of Physical Medicine and Rehabilitation, 69,* 678-681.

Lahm, E., & Elting, S. (1989). Technology: Becoming an informed consumer. *National Information Center for Children and Youth with Handicaps News Digest, 13,* 1-3.

Lehman, L.B. (1990). Intracranial pressure monitoring and treatment: A contemporary view. *Annals of Emergency Medicine, 19,* 295-303.

Lehr, E. (1991, February). Neuropsychological evaluation of children after TBI: Assessment and management issues. Paper presented at Visions Becoming Reality: A conference on advances and treatment in pediatric neurological disorders. Sarasota, FL.

Leigh, A.D. (1943). Defects of smell after head injury. *Lancet, 1,* 38-40.

Leiner, H.C., Leiner, A.L., & Dow, R.S. (1986). Does the cerebellum contribute to mental skills? *Behavioral Neuroscience, 100,* 443-454.

Levin, H.S., (1990). Cognitive rehabilitation. *Archives of Neurology, 47,* 223-224.

Levin, H.S., Amparo, E., Eisenberg, H.M., Williams, D.H., High, W.M., Jr., McArdle, C.B., & Weiner, R.L. (1987). Magnetic resonance imaging and computerized tomograpy in relation to the neurobehavioral sequelae of mild and moderate head injuries. *Journal of Neurosurgery, 66,* 706-713.

Levin, H.S., O'Donnell, V.M., & Grossman, R.G. (1979). The Galveston Orientation and Amnesia Test: A practical scale to assess cognition after head injury. *Journal of Nervous and Mental Diseases, 167,* 675-684.

Lewis, D.D., Pincus, J.H., Feldman, M., Jackson, L., & Bard, B. (1986). Psychiatric, neurological, and psychoeducational characteristics of 15 death row inmates in the United States. *American Journal of Psychiatry, 143,* 838-845.

Lewis, D.D., Shanok, S.S., & Balla, D.A. (1979). Perinatal difficulties, head and face trauma, and child abuse in the medical histories of seriously delinquent children. *American Journal of Psychiatry, 136,* 419-423.

Lezak, M.D. (1982). The problem of assessing executive functions. *International Journal of Psychology, 17,* 281-297.

Light, J., Beesley, M., & Collier, B. (1988). Transition through multiple augmentative and alternative communication systems: A three-year case study of a head injured adolescent. *AAC Augmentative and Alternative Communication, 4*(1), 2-14.

Lishman, W.A. (1968). Brain damage in relation to psychiatric disability after head injury. *British Journal of Psychiatry, 114,* 373-410.

Malkmus, D., Booth, P.J., & Kodimer, C. (1980). *Rehabilitation of the head injured adult: Comprehensive cognitive management.* Downey, CA: Rancho Los Amigos Hospital, Inc.

Mattson, A.J., & Levin, H.S. (1990). Frontal lobe dysfunction following closed head injury. *Journal of Nervous and Mental Diseases, 178,* 282-291.

Mira, M.P., Meck, N.E., & Tyler, J.S. (1988). School psychologist's knowledge of traumatic head injury: Implications for training. *Diagnostique, 13,* 174-180.

Mitchell, S., Bradley, V.A., Welch, J.L., & Britton, P.G. (1990). Coma arousal procedure: A therapeutic intervention in the treatment of head injury. *Brain Injury, 4*(3), 273-279.

Murray, G.B. (1985, April). Psychiatric disorders secondary to complex partial seizures. *Drug Therapy*, 21-26.

Ommaya, A.K. (1966). Trauma to the nervous system. *Annals of the Royal College of Surgeons of England*, *39*, 317-347.

Pierce, J.P., Lyle, D.M., Quine, S., Evans, N.J., Morris, J., & Fearnside, M.R. (1990). The effectiveness of coma arousal intervention. *Brain Injury*, *4*(2), 191-197.

Plum, F., & Posner, J.B. (1966, 1987). *Diagnosis of stupor and coma* (1st & 3rd eds.). Philadelphia: F.A. Davis.

Rappaport, M., Hall, K.M., Hopkins, K., Belleza, T., & Cope, N. (1982). Disability Rating Scale for severe head trauma. *Archives of Physical Medicine and Rehabilitation*, *63*, 118-123.

Reitan, H.M. (1969). *Manual for the administration of neuropsychological test batteries for children and adults*. Tucson, AZ: Neuropsychology Laboratory.

Rhein, B., & Farmer, H. (1991, September). Teaching strategies for students with traumatic brain injuries. Paper presented at the 5th Annual Conference on Cognitive Rehabilitation and Community Integration, Virginia Beach, VA.

Rimel, R.W., Giordani, B., Barth, J.T., Boll, T.J., & Jane, J.A. (1981). Disability caused by minor head injury. *Neurosurgery*, *9*, 221-228.

Rimel, R.W., Giordani, B., Barth, J.T., & Jane, J.A. (1982). Moderate head injury: Completing the clinical spectrum of brain trauma. *Neurosurgery*, *11*, 344-351.

Rinehart, M.A. (1983). Considerations for functional training of adults after head injury. *Physical Therapy*, *63*, 1975-1982.

Robbins, D.M., Beck, J.C., Pries, R., Jacobs, D., & Smith, C. (1983). Learning disability and neuropsychological impairment in adjudicated, unincarcerated male delinquents. *Journal of the American Academy of Child Psychiatry*, *22*, 40-46.

Rosman, N.P., & Oppenheimer, E.Y. (1982). Posttraumatic epilepsy. *Pediatrics in Review*, *3*, 221-225.

Russell, W.R. (1932). Cerebral involvement in head injury. *Brain*, *55*, 549-603.

Rutter, M. (1981). Psychological sequelae of brain damage in children. *American Journal of Psychiatry*, *138*, 1533-1544.

Savage, R.C. (1991). Identification, classification, and placement issues for students with traumatic brain injuries. *Journal of Head Trauma Rehabilitation*, *6*(1), 1-9.

Savage, R.C., & Carter, R.R. (1988). Transitioning pediatric patients into educational systems: Guidelines for rehabilitation professionals. *Cognitive Rehabilitation*, *6*(4), 10-14.

Savage, R.C., & Wolcott, G. (Eds.). (1988). *An educator's manual: What educators need to know about students with traumatic brain injury*. Baltimore: P.H. Brookes

Sazbon, L., & Groswasser, Z. (1991). Prolonged coma, vegetative state, post-comatose unawareness: Semantics or better understanding? *Brain Injury*, *5*(1), 1-2.

Schwartz, R. (1989, August). Early rehabilitation in trauma centers: Have speech-language pathology services progressed? A 3 year follow-up. *Asha*, 91-94.

Schwartz-Cowley, R., & Stepanik, M.J. (1989). Communication disorders and treatment in the acute trauma center setting. *Topics in Language Disorders*, *9*(2), 1-14.

Shaffer, D., Bijur, P., Chadwick, O.F.D., & Rutter, M.L. (1980). Head injury and later reading disability. *Journal of the American Academy of Child Psychiatry, 19,* 592-610.

Soderstrom, C.A. (1982). Severe pelvic fractures: Problems and possible solutions. *American Surgeon, 48,* 441-446.

Sohlberg, M.M., & Mateer, C.A. (1989a). The assessment of cognitive communicative functions in head injury. *Topics in Language Disorders, 9*(2), 15-33.

Sohlberg, M.M., & Mateer, C.A. (1989b). *Introduction to cognitive rehabilitation: Theory and practice.* New York: Guilford Press.

Stepanik, M.J., & Roth, W. (1985). Certain aspects of post-traumatic aphasia. Paper presented at the annual meeting of the Maryland Head Injury Foundation, Baltimore.

Stevens, M.M. (1984). *Post concussion syndrome.* National Head Injury Foundation pamphlet. Available from National Head Injury Foundation Inc., P.O. Box 567, Framingham, MA 01701

Stuss, D.T., & Benson, D.F. (1987). The frontal lobes and control of cognition and memory. In E. Perecman (Ed.), *The frontal lobes revisited.* New York: The IRBN Press.

Talmage, E.W., & Collins, G.A. (1983). Physical abilities after head injury. A retrospective study. *Physical Therapy, 63,* 2010-2015.

Teasdale, G., & Jennett, B. (1974). Assessment of coma and impaired consciousness. *Lancet, 2,* 81-84

Telzrow, C.F. (1991). The school psychologist's perspective on testing students with traumatic brain injury. *Journal of Head Trauma Rehabilitation, 6*(1), 23-34.

Temkin, N.R., Dikmen, S.S., Wilensky, A.J., Keihm, J., Chabal, S.,& Winn, H.R. (1990). A randomized double-blind study of phenytoin for the prevention of post-traumatic seizures. *The New England Journal of Medicine, 323,* 497-502.

Thompson, L.L., & Filley, C.M. (1989). A pilot study of neuropsychological rehabilitation. *Journal of Neurological Rehabilitation, 3,* 117-127.

Thomsen, I.V. (1984). Late outcome of very severe blunt head trauma: A 10-15 year second follow-up. *Journal of Neurology, Neurosurgery, and Psychiatry, 47,* 260-268.

Tsubokawa, T., Yamamoto, T., Katayama, Y., Hirayama, T., Maejima, S., & Moriya, T. (1990). Deep-brain stimulation in a persistent vegetative state: Follow-up results and criteria for selection of candidates. *Brain Injury, 4*(4), 315-327.

Tyler, J.S. (1990). *Traumatic head injury in school age children: A training manual for educational personnel.* Kansas City: University of Kansas Medical Center.

U.S. Congress, Public Law 94-142. Education for all Handicapped Children Act of 1975. Washington, DC: U.S. Government Printing Office.

U.S. Congress, Public Law 99-457, The Education of the Handicapped Act Amendments of 1986. Washington, DC: U.S. Government Printing Office.

U.S. Congress, Public Law 101-476, Individuals with Disabilities Education Act of 1989. Washington, DC: U.S. Government Printing Office.

Volpe, B.T., Fletcher, H., & McDowell, F.H. (1990). The efficacy of cognitive rehabilitation in patients with traumatic brain injury. *Archives of Neurology, 47,* 220-222.

Welsh, M.C., Pennington, B.F., & Grossier, D.B. (1991). A normative developmental study of executive function: A window on prefrontal function in children. *Developmental Neuropsychology, 7*(2) 131-149.

Wilds, M.L. (1989). Effective use of technology with young children. *National Information Center for Children and Youth with Handicaps News Digest, 13,* 6-7.

Willmore, L.J. (1990). Post-traumatic epilepsy: Cellular mechanisms and implications for treatment. *Epilepsy, 31*(Suppl. 3), S67-S73.

Wilson, J.T.L., Wiedmann, K.D., Hadley, D.M., Condon, B., Teasdale, G. & Brooks, D.N. (1988). Early and late magnetic resonance imaging and neuropsychological outcome after head injury. *Journal of Neurology, Neurosurgery, and Psychiatry, 51,* 391-396.

Zimmerman, R.A., & Bilaniuk, L.T. (1989). CT and MR: Diagnosis and evolution of head injury, stroke, and brain tumors. *Neuropsychology, 3,* 191-230.

Glossary

anomia: a naming impairment that is the most common linguistic deficit following closed-head trauma. A test for naming ability as a component of oral expression is included in aphasia batteries.

aphasia: a term that includes various deficits in the expressive and receptive aspects of language. Aphasia may be diagnosed clinically or by means of a standardized battery of tests. The diagnosis in a child who has not yet attained mature language function may be difficult. Language impairment after severe closed-head injury in children and adolescents is a combination of aphasia and a global cognitive deficit that follows the injury.

ataxia: a failure of muscular coordination that results in impaired balance, tremors, and dysarthric speech. It is a common motor impairment following severe closed-head injury, caused by damage to the cerebellum or to sensory tracts that regulate coordination of movement.

coma: a state of unconsciousness and behavioral unresponsiveness. The depth and duration of coma are important indicators of prognosis in closed-head injury. Termination of coma is commonly measured by attainment of a simple command level by the patient.

computerized tomography, or **CT scanning**: a rapid, noninvasive X-ray method of visualizing the inside of an organ and the extent of disease. The technique has been adapted for use with many organs, including the brain. Performance of a brain CT is the procedure of choice in the first few days after head injury, as the scan is easy to perform and it best distinguishes areas of hemorrhage that can be removed by surgery.

disinhibition: a lack of control that contributes to a number of maladaptive behaviors seen after head injury. These behaviors are attributed to frontal lobe dysfunction, and include carelessness in hygiene and dress, inappropriate words or acts, overtalkativeness, and hyperphagia. Disinhibition tends to lessen over time and may respond to conditioning methods.

dysarthria: an oral-motor speech impairment that is due to muscular incoordination. Dysarthria is often seen in combination with an expressive or receptive language deficit.

edema: the excessive accumulation of fluid, both intracellular and extra-cellular, that occurs in the brain as a result of closed-head injury. The acute mechanical and drug treatment of closed-head injury aims to remove edema fluid and to decrease its formation.

electroencephalogram (EEG): a measure of brain electrical activity using a standard arrangement of electrodes attached to the scalp. The process is painless and is performed while the patient is in both sleep and wake states. Abnormality is defined as deviation from normal patterns. After head trauma, EEG readings are often grossly abnormal for varying periods. EEGs have not proved to be very helpful in the prediction of posttraumatic epilepsy.

Glasgow Coma Scale: a widely used, easily administered intensive care clinical scale that measures the depth and duration of unconsciousness. Three components (eye opening, verbal ability, and motor ability) are scored and then combined into a composite score of from 3 to 15. A patient with an initial Glasgow Coma Scale score of 8 or lower is usually admitted to a specialized intensive care unit.

hematoma: an abnormal blood collection occurring when trauma damages cerebral blood vessels, that is diagnosed by CT scan and MRI. These blood collections cause damage by occupying space and causing pressure on adjacent structures. Many hematomas must be removed by neurosurgical procedures to prevent compromise of vital structures. Occasionally, a small hematoma may be simply observed by sequential scanning until resolution occurs or it is certain that its presence poses no danger.

hemiparesis: See **paresis**.

hemiplegia: See **paralysis**.

hydrocephalus: an abnormal amount of fluid in the ventricular system, which may occur as a complication of closed-head injury. The ventricles will appear dilated on CT scan and MRI. This condition must be distinguished from cerebral atrophy with secondary dilatation of the ventricles. If hydrocephalus is diagnosed and is caused by an obstruction, then the cerebrospinal fluid can be shunted from the ventricular system to a blood vessel to relieve the build-up of fluid.

hypertension: elevation of systemic blood pressure. Hypertension is more common and tends to last longer in patients with histories of prolonged coma.

intracranial pressure (ICP): the exertion of force upon structures within the brain by a combination of intracellular and extracellular fluids. Maintenance of intracranial pressure in the normal range is a central focus of intensive care after closed-head injury. Heightened ICP damages the brain by causing mechanical distortion or displacement of cerebral structures or reduction in cerebral blood flow. ICP may be continuously monitored by devices that are inserted into the space surrounding the brain. Medication and other treatments may be administered in response to pressure changes.

magnetic resonance imaging or MRI: a neuroimaging procedure introduced in 1982 that utilizes differences in magnetic fields to visualize internal organs and does not entail the use of radiation. After the first few days from the time of injury, MRI becomes the most sensitive technique to detect brain abnormalities such as tissue disruption, hemorrhage, and white matter injury.

neurointensive care: interdisciplinary care of severe neurologic illnesses carried out in specialized clinical units in major medical centers. These units are characterized by a high staff-patient ratio, advanced technologic instruments, and a great degree of expertise in pharmacologic management.

neuropsychology: the branch of psychology that tests different specific components of cognition by examining elements such as memory, visuoperceptual function, and reaction time. The neuropsychologist is interested in determining the site and mechanism of damage to specific functions. The specialist works with other members of the acute and postacute rehabilitation treatment teams to devise specific remediation strategies for the head-injured patient.

paralysis: neurologic muscular dysfunction to the extent of immobility. With lack of movement, muscles begin to contract and become smaller or atrophic. Paralysis of the extremities on one side of the body is called hemiplegia. Paralysis of all four extremities is called quadriplegia.

paresis: increased muscle tone secondary to damage to brain pathways regulating movement. Hemiparesis is increased muscle tone of the extremities on one side of the body. Quadriparesis is increased tone of all four extremities.

persistent vegetative state: the most severe sequela of severe closed-head injury, occurring in less than 5% of survivors. Heart and lungs function independently in this condition. The patient may move limbs, swallow, and make sounds. He or she has periods of apparent sleep and wakefulness and the EEG may show normal alpha rhythms. The patient remains in a state of behavioral unresponsiveness, however, with no indication of mental functioning.

posttraumatic amnesia: the period of time after head injury during which the patient has no continuous memories. This period consists of the coma and the period of anterograde amnesia, measured by sequential tests of orientation and memory.

posttraumatic epilepsy: a type of seizure disorder occurring in greater than 5% of patients who suffer closed-head injury. The incidence of post-traumatic epilepsy is up to 25% after open-head injury. The more severe the injury, the greater the likelihood that seizures will appear. Seizures may consist of motor or sensory activity or emotional states or may be a combination of these.

rehabilitation: The process by which people with disabilities and handicaps are helped to make maximum use of their abilities and to achieve satisfaction and usefulness in their daily lives. Physical and mental exercises are used in graduated programs to encourage return of damaged functions. These programs are devised and administered in an inter-disciplinary model by trained professionals in physical, cognitive, and psychologic specialties.

severe closed-head injury: blunt head injury causing damage by impact but not penetrating the brain or its protective coverings. Closed-head injury is more likely to result in unconsciousness than open head injury, while open-head injury more likely serves as an entry for infection. Severe closed-head injury may be defined as 6 or more hours of unconsciousness or by an admission Glasgow Coma Scale score of 3 to 8.

ventricles: cavities inside the brain which form a system of passage for the cerebrospinal fluid that circulates over and inside the brain. The spinal fluid serves as a protective cushion and carries nutrients and wastes to and from the blood. Enlargement of the ventricles after head injury may indicate an obstruction to the flow of spinal fluid, or, more commonly, is an indication of diffuse loss of cerebral substance.

visuoperceptual function: a person's visual interpretation of shapes, sizes, distances, and locations of objects, as well as recognition of faces. The Bender Gestalt Test and tests of facial recognition are instruments that evaluate visuoperceptual function.

Subject Index

Abnormalities, acute, on MRI, 9
Aggression, 58, 59
  in hospital, 21
  premorbid history, 25-26
  treatment, behavioral, 24
Airway obstruction, 8
Ambulation, 41, 42, 43. See Also
    Motor impairment
  exercise, 44
Amnesia, 66
  anterograde, 14
  posttraumatic. See *PTA*
  retrograde, 14
Amnestic syndrome, 147
Anatomy, brain, 1-6
Anger, posttraumatic, 17
Anterograde amnesia. See
    Amnesia, anterograde
Apathy, 58
Aphasia, 3-4, 52
Appetite regulation, 4
Apraxia, 3-4
Architectural barriers, school, 90
Assessment, 45
  achievement, 101
  areas, 106
  attention, 45, 107
  Bender Gestalt Test, 48-49
  COAT, 15-16, 151-153
  cognitive rehabilitation, 37-38
  concentration, 45
  Controlled Oral Word
    Association Test, 50
  Disability Rating Scale, 55-56
  discharge goals, 35
  educational, 101-111

educational overview, 101-111
executive functions, 50, 108
& family, 35, 108, 109
functional outcome measures,
  54-56
Glascow Coma Scale, 8, 81, 134,
  155-156
Glasgow Outcome Scale, 54-55
GOAT, 15-16
informal samples, 107-108
& instructional strategies, 110
intelligence, 101
interpretation, 109-111
memory, 45
Minnesota Computerized
  Assessment, 50
motor impairment, 43
motor speed, 45
multidisciplinary, 104-105
neurobehavioral factors, 109
neuropsychologic, 36, 45-47
& pretrauma functioning, 35,
  108-109
Rancho Los Amigos Levels of
  Cognitive Functioning
  Scale, 53, 81, 134, 155-
  156
rehabilitation, 34-35
selection/test instruments, 106-
  107
severity, early, 13
test manual adaptation, 107
timing of, 104-105
Tower of Hanoi, 50
verbal, 49-50, 50
visuomotor, 45

Assessment (cont.)
  visuospatial, 45, 49-50
  Wisconsin Card Sorting Test,
      49-50
Assignments
  classroom, 70
  long-term, 72
Astereognosis, 3-4
Ataxia, 5, 44, 125-126
  & rehabilitation, 40-41
Atrophy prevention, muscle, 19
Attention, 49, 107, 116-117
  assessment, 45
Audiologist, 36
Audiotapes & educational reentry,
    70
Auditory, 3, 118-119
Axonal injury, 6

Barriers
  logistical, 90
  noninstructional, 85
  school architectural, 90
Behavioral impairment. See
    Psychiatric
Behavior management, 126-129
Bender Gestalt Test, 48-49
Bleeding
  closed-head injury, 6
  intracranial, CT scan, 9
Blindness, 19-20
Blood clots, CT scan, 9
Blood pressure, 4, 21
Blunt injury. See *Closed-head
    injury*
Brain anatomy, 1-6
Brain lacerations, 6
Brainstem, 2, 3, 4, 20, 59
  lesions, 6
Brainstem damage, severe, 4
Brain tissue loss, diffuse, 47
Breathing problems, 10, 12

Canes, 44
Carbon dioxide, high, 6
Care coordinator. See *Case
    manager*
Case management
  case manager, 37
  educational reentry, 95
  preschoolers, 99
Central nervous system, 1, 5-6
  tract crossover, 1-2

Charting, emergency care, 8
Chewing, rehabilitation, 44
Childishness, 58
Children's Orientation and
    Amnesia Test (COAT), 15-
    16, 151-153
Circulation problems, 10
Classroom strategies, 113-138
  attention, 116-117
  auditory deficits, 118-119
  comprehension deficits, 120-122
  conduct deficits, 126-129
  disorientation, 117-118
  & family, 143
  fatigue, 130
  fire drills, 142
  independent functioning
      deficits, 125
  information processing, 118
  insight deficits, 129-131
  listening deficits, 121-122
  mathematics, 121
  memory, 123-124
  mental flexibility deficits, 124-
      125
  organization deficits, 122
  physical adaptation, 131
  reading, 120-121
  reasoning deficits, 124-125
  seizures, 141
  sensory deficits, 118-120
  suicide, 130-131
  visual deficits, 119-120
  writing, 125-126
Closed-head injury
  adolescent, 25-26
  age & prognosis, 16
  auditory impairment, 20
  axonal injury, 6
  bleeding, 6
  blindness, 19-20
  blood pressure, 6
  brain lacerations, 6
  child, mild & moderate, 32-33
  contusions, 6
  deficit predictability, 6
  dizziness, 20
  equilibrium loss, 20
  eyelid drooping, 20
  fractures, 20-21
  gray matter lesions, 6
  hallucinations, 23
  hemorrhage, 21

Closed-head injury (*cont.*)
  high carbon dioxide, 6
  hospital mortality, 13
  hypertension, 21
  intercranial pressure, 6
  internal injuries, 20
  lesions, 6
  low oxygen, 6
  mild, 13
  moderate, 13
  motor impairment, 19
  olfactory deficit, 20
  paralysis, 6
  patient inattention, 22-23
  pediatric, 13, 16, 19
  personality changes, 57
  prehospital mortality, 13
  primary vs. secondary, 6
  psychiatric prognosis, 56-57
  pupil size, 20
  seizures, 6
  sensory impairment, 19-20
  severe, 13, 15
  strabismus, 20
  vessel tears, 6
Cognitive disorganization,
      language deficits, 52
Cognitive functioning, 110
Cognitive impairment, 45-50. See
      Also *Neuropsychology*
Cognitive rehabilitation. See
      Neuropsychology,
      Psychiatric
Coma, 12-14, 129
  acute inpatient rehabilitation, 34
  awakening, 21
  breathing, 12
  duration, 12, 13-14
  emergence & overactivity, 23
  emergency care, 8
  end defined, 12
  exercise, 41
  eye signs, 12
  immediate, 12-14
  & intellectual impairment, 45
  muteness, 50
  neuropsychological deficits, 47
  recovery, 12-13
  sleep-wake cycle, 22
  speech return, 12-13
Communication
  computer aids, 54
  discharge goals, 37

Communication boards, 54
Community resources, referrals, 92
Computerized Tomography. See
      CT scan
Computers, classroom, 126, 132,
      133
Concentration, assessment, 45
Concentration deficits, 49
Confabulation, 51
Consciousness regulation, 4
Contracture prevention, muscle,
      19
Contrecoup injury, 6
Controlled Oral Word Association
      Test, 50
Counseling, 78, 84, 130
CT scan, 9
CT scan diagnosis,
      neuropsychological deficits,
      9, 47

Deficit continuum, 101-103
Deficit-injury site correlation,
      MRI, 46
Deficits, 102
  ambulation, 131
  attention, 116-117
  auditory, 102, 118-119
  cognitive, 115
  communication, 115
  compliance, 103
  comprehension, 120-122
  concentration, 49
  conduct, 126-129
  demandingness, 58
  disinhibition, 56, 58, 59, 67,
      126-129
  disorientation, 66, 117-118
  disruptive behavior, 21, 66
  executive functions, 125
  fatigue, 130
  hemiparesis, 131
  independent functioning, 125
  information processing, 118
  insight, 129-131
  judgment, 102
  listening, 121-122
  math, 102, 121
  memory, 3, 123-124
  mental flexibility, 124-125
  mood, 103
  motivation, 102
  organizational skills, 122

Deficits (*cont.*)
  psychiatric, 15
  reading, 102, 120-121
  reasoning, 124-125
  self-control, 103
  self-esteem, 103
  self-monitoring, 103
  sensory, 115, 118-120
  speech, 131
  thinking, 102
  visual, 102, 119-120
  writing, 102, 125-126
Delinquent behavior, 60
Delirium, 21-22, 147
Dementia, 147
Denial, & rehabilitation, 27-28
Depression, 28, 51
  postconcussion, 59
  & seizure, 17
Diagnosis, early, 8-10
*Diagnostic and Statistic Manual
     IV*, proposed, 147
Diencephalon, 4
Disability, severe, 56
Discharge, rehabilitation, 92-99
Discharge goals, 37
  in-patient, 35
Discharge planning,
     neuropsychology, 47
Discharge to home, 66
Disinhibition, 56, 58, 67
Disorientation, 66
Disruptive behaviors, 21, 66
Distractibility, 58, 71
Dizziness, postconcussion, 59
Drivers' education, 141
Drug treatment, early, 11
Dysarthria, 41, 51, 56
Dysfluency, 51
Dysphagia, 39, 41

Edema, 9, 10-12
Educational deficits, memory, 47-48
Educational intervention, 72
Educational planning,
     posttraumatic, 63-79
Educational reentry
  ancillary services, 83-84
  audiotapes, 70
  case management, 95
  common problems, 82-86
  counseling, 84
  demand reduction, 69-71

drivers' education, 141
  flexibility, 69
  home economics, 142
  industrial arts, 142
  inservice training, 94, 97-98
  interagency relations, 82-83
  medically fragile youngster, 98
  mild head trauma, 98
  missed instruction, 68-69
  noise level, 140
  optimal placement, 74-75
  parents, 70
  peer preparation, 140
  physical education, 140
  rehabilitation interaction, 90-91
  rehabilitation liaison, 86-90
  return to same class, 78-79
  social readjustment, 142-143
  & treatment differences, 65-67
  year-round programming, 86
Education of the Handicapped
     Act. See *Public Law 94-142*
Education of the Handicapped
     Amendments of 1986, 99
Education specialist, hospital-
     based, 86-90
EEG, 17
EHA. See *Public Law 94-142*
Electroencephalogram. See *EEG*
Elementary school supervision,
     71-72
Eligibility, special education, 104
Emergency care, 8-9
Emotional impairment. See
     Psychiatric
Emotional lability, postconcussion,
     59
Epilepsy, 9
  posttraumatic. See *Seizure*
Equilibrium maintenance, 4-5
Euphoria, 58
Executive functions, 2-3, 49. See
     Also *Anticipation,
     Organization, Goal selection*
  assessment, 50
Exercise
  ambulation, 44
  & coma, 41
  & immobile patients, 43
Extracranial injuries, 18-19
Eye patterns
  coma, 12
  Glasgow Coma Scale, 13

Family
  amnesia, posttraumatic, 26-30
  & assessment, 108, 109
  assessment input, 35
  & classroom strategies, 115-116
  community resource referral, 92
  rehabilitation interaction, 91-92
  viewpoint, 143-144
Fatigue, postconcussion, 59
Fearfulness, 21
Feeding, & rehabilitation, 39
Fine motor deficits, 49
Fire drills, 142
Flashbacks, 29
Fractures, 21, 34
Frontal lobe injury, 1, 3, 49-50,
  58-59, 125, 128
Functional adjustment, 58

Galveston Orientation and
  Amnesia Test (GOAT), 15-16
Gas analysis, blood, 8
Gastrostomy tube, 39
Glasgow Coma Scale, 8, 11, 13,
  59, 149
  eye opening, 13
  initial score, 16
  motor ability, 13
  scores, 13
  verbal ability, 13
Glasgow Outcome Scale, 54-55
Gray matter, hemorrhage, 6
Guidance counselor, 78, 84, 130

Hallucination, 3, 17, 23
Headache, postconcussion, 59
Heart rate regulation, 4
Helmets as protection, 141
Hematoma, CT scan, 9
Hematomas, MRI, 9
Hemiparesis, 19, 131
Hemorrhage, 6, 21
Herniation, 10-11
Hippocampus, 4
Home economics, 142
Home instruction, 76-77
Home-school combination, 77
Homonymous hemianopia, 20
Hospital to home
  early school reentry, 72-75
  educator expectations, 74
  parental expectations, 73-74
  services available, 73-76

timing, 72-73
Hyperactivity, 18, 58

ICP. See *Intracranial pressure,*
  raised
IDEA. See *Public Law 101-476*
Illusions. See *Hallucinations*
Imbalance, 40
Impulsivity, 59
Inattention, 58
Individualized Educational
  Program, 83, 86, 93-94, 105.
  See Also *Public Law 94-*
  142, Public Law 101-476
Individuals with Disabilities
  Education Act. See *Public*
  Law 101-142
Industrial arts, 142
Infants and Toddlers Program
  (Part H), 99
Information processing deficits, 48
Injury vulnerability, frontal lobe, 2
Inservice training, educational, 94,
  97-98
Insomnia, postconcussion, 59
Intellectual impairment, 45
Interagency relations, 82-83
Intercranial pressure high, 6
Interdisciplinary cooperation, 145-
  146
Interdisciplinary team,
  rehabilitation, 35-38
Interpersonal functions, 2-3
Intracranial blood pressure
  monitoring, 8
Intracranial pressure, raised, 11-12

Jaw wiring, & rehabilitation, 21

Language, 2, 3
Language deficits
  affective prosody, 51
  aphasia, 52
  & cognitive disorganization, 52
  dysarthria, 41, 51, 56
  dysfluency, 51
  long-term, 51-52
  sparse production, 51
  verbosity, 51
Language recovery, 50-52
Learning problems, pretrauma, 65
Lesions, 6
Limbic system, 4

Listening comprehension, 70

Magnetic Resonance Imaging. See
    MRI
Mandated public education, 74-76
Mathematics, 64-65, 121
Medically fragile youngsters,
    education, 98
Medication, 18, 24
    & activity level, 23-24
    aggression, 24
    antiseizure, 18
    blood pressure, 21
    carbamazepine, 25
    & coma emergence, 24
    hallucinations, 23
    haloperidol, 25
    lithium, 25
    pediatric, 18
    prophylactic, 18
    propranolol, 25
    seizure, 18
    sleep-wake cycle, 22
    thioridazine, 24
    toxicity, 18
Memory, 2, 3, 46, 59
    assessment, 45
    & classroom, 123-124
    deficits, 47-48, 123-124
    evaluation, 115
    long-term recall, 47
    short-term, deficits, 15
Mild-and-moderate injury,
    neuropsychological deficits,
    47
Minnesota Computerized
    Assessment, 50
Mnemonic cues, classroom, 70
Motor ability, Glascow Coma
    Scale, 13
Motor impairment, 19
    assessment, 43
    & rehabilitation, 40-44
    treatment, 41-44
Motor speed
    assessment, 45
    deficits, 49
MRI
    abnormalities, late, 47
    acute abnormalities, 9
    correlation injury site & deficit,
    46
Multiple injury diagnosis, 8

Muscle activation, 5
Muscle atrophy prevention, 19
Muscle contracture prevention, 19
Muscle tone maintenance, 4-5

Naiveté, student, 71
Neuroimaging, 9
Neurologic status, early, 8
Neurology, 35
Neuropsychiatry, 21-26
Neuropsychological, assessment,
    45-47
Neuropsychological deficits
    & coma duration, 47
    & CT scan diagnosis, 47
    long-term memory recall, 47
    mild-and-moderate injury, 47
    premorbid predictors, 47
    ventricular enlargement, 47
    verbal recall, 47
    visual memory, 47
    visuospatial recall, 47
Neuropsychology, 33, 36, 46, 104.
    See Also *Cognitive
    impairment*
    discharge planning, 47
    frontal lobe, 49-50
    MRI, 46
New learning, educational, 114-
    116
Nightmares, 29
Noninstructional barriers, 85
Notetaking & head injury, 70-71
Nutrition, discharge goals, 37
Nutritionist, 36

Occupational deficits, memory,
    47-48
Occupational therapy, 31, 32, 36,
    41, 43-44, 84, 104, 145
Olfactory deficit, 20
Orthotic devices, 44
Oxygen, low, 6

Paranoia, 3, 59
Parietal lesions, 3-4
Parietal lobe, 3
Parosmia, 20
Pediatric
    closed-head injury, 13
    extracranial injuries, 19
    injuries, 16
    seizure, 17-18

Pediatrician, 82
Peer, rehabilitation interaction, 91-
    92
Persistent vegetative state, 56
    educational strategies, 132-135
    sensory stimulation, 136-138
Personal hygiene lack, 59
Physiatry, 31, 35
Physical education, 140
Physical therapy, 19, 31, 32, 36,
    41, 42, 44, 84, 104, 145
Plastic surgery, 40
Postconcussion syndrome, 59-60
Postemergency care, 9-30
Posttraumatic amnesia. See *PTA*
Posttraumatic epilepsy. See
    Seizure
Posttraumatic psychosis. See
    Psychiatric
Posttraumatic stress disorder, 28-
    30
Pretrauma
    academic level, 105
    functioning & assessment, 108-
        109
Problem solving, aphasia, 64-65
Prosody, affective deficits, 51
Psychiatric
    acute inpatient rehabilitation, 57
    classification, 147-148
    diagnosis, 21-22
    impairment, 56-61
Psychiatric impairment
    delirium, 57
    frontal lobe, 58-59
    likelihood, 58
    mild-and-moderate head injury,
        59
    predictability, 15
    & pretraumatic personality
        traits, 57-58
    temporal lobe, 58
    treatment, 60-61
Psychiatry, 33, 35-36, 61. See
    Also *Neuropsychiatric*
Psychologist, 130
    behavioral, 35-36, 61
    hospital-based, 86
Psychotherapy, 30
PTA, 14-15, 21
    activity levels, 23-25
    acute-care discharge, 31
    aggressive behavior, 23-26

anger, 27-28
assessment, 15-16
child overactivity, 24
denial, 27-28
as diagnostic measure, 14-15
duration, 14-15
& family, 26-30
hallucinations, 23
& intellectual impairment, 45
& learning, 35
sleep, 26
sleep-wake cycle, 22
speech resumption, 51-52
spontaneous recovery, 35
PTSD. See *Posttraumatic stress
    disorder*
Public Law 94-142, 74, 75, 76, 83,
    99
Public Law 99-457, 99
Public Law 101-476, 74-75, 83

Quadriparesis, 19

Rancho Los Amigos Level of
    Cognitive Functioning
    Scale, 53
Rancho Los Amigos Levels of
    Cognitive Functioning, 81,
    134, 155-156
Reading, 120-121
Reading comprehension,
    posttraumatic, 64
Reading recognition,
    posttraumatic, 64
Recovery
    early, 7-30
    long-term, 31-62
    prognosis, 81-82
    spontaneous, 33
Recreation therapy, 36, 61
Reentry, community, postacute, 32
Rehabilitation
    adult postacute, 33-34
    ambulation, 21
    assessment, 34-35
    & ataxia, 40-41
    case management, 95
    chewing, 44
    child postacute, 34
    cognitive. See *Neuropsychology,
        Psychiatric*
    cognitive assessment, 36-37
    & coma, 34

Rehabilitation (*cont.*)
  denial, family, 28
  discharge planning, 86-90
  discharge timing, 92
  & dysphagia, 39
  eating, 41
  family interaction, 91-92
  & feeding, 39
  & fractures, 21
  & fracture treatment, 34
  grooming, 41
  inpatient education, 37-38
  in-patient vs. out-patient, 32
  interdisciplinary team, 35-38
  medical problems, 38-40
  & motor impairment, 40-44
  multidisplinary evaluation, 93
  neuropsychology, 33
  occupational therapy, 32
  peer interaction, 91-92
  perceptual skills, 41
  physical therapy, 32
  postacute, 31-34
  postacute in-patient, 32
  postacute & schools, 32-33
  psychiatric, 33
  psychologic resources, 26
  & scarring, 40
  school coordination, 37-38
  school interaction, 90-91
  & school reentry, 86-90
  sibling interaction, 91-92
  social work, 32
  & spasticity, 40
  special education, 32, 34
  & special educator, 37-38
  speech/language, 21
  speech-language therapy, 32
  swallowing, 44
  & tracheostomy, 38-39
Rehabilitation impact on
    education, 66-67
Rehabilitation medicine. See
    Physiatry
Rehabilitation therapist, 87-91
Residental schools, 75
Respiratory status, early, 8
Reteaching, 114-116
Retrograde amnesia. See *Amnesia,
    retrograde*
Review, educational, 114-116

Scarring, & rehabilitation, 40
School, postacute rehabilitation,
    32-33
School environment, least
    restrictive, 75
School program
  modified, 77-78
  reduced, 77
School reentry, staff preplanning,
    75
Schools, & outside agencies, 34
Secondary injury, 6
Secondary school supervision, 71-
    72
Sedation, 18
Seizure, 3, 16-18, 141
  classroom, 18
  closed-head vs. open-head
      injury, 17
  convulsive, 17
  & injury severity, 17-18
  medication, 18
  nonconvulsive, 17
  occurrence later, 18
  partial, 17
  pediatric, 17-18
  treatment, 18
Self-regulating functions, 49-50.
    See Also *Attention*
Sensation, 2
Sensorimotor functioning, 110
Sensorimotor impairment, 107
Sensory apraxia, 3-4
Sensory association, 3
Sensory stimulation, 136-138
Sibling, rehabilitation interaction,
    91-92
Siblings, amnesia, posttraumatic,
    26
Sleep, anxiety dreams, 26
Sleep-wake cycle, 22
Social discourse functions, 2-3
Social readjustment, 142-143
Social work, 32
Social worker, 36, 61, 104
Somatosensory deficits, 48-49
Sound sensitivity, postconcussion,
    59
Spasticity, 19, 44
  & rehabilitation, 40
Spastic paralysis, 56

Special classes, 75
Special education, 32, 78
  eligibility, 83-84, 104
  meeting head-injury needs, 83-84
  rehabilitation, postacute, 34
Special educator, 36
  inpatient rehabilitation, 37-38
Speech
  coma recovery, 12-13
  Glasgow Coma Scale, 13
Speech association, 3
Speech deficits, confabulation, 51
Speech-language. See Also
    Communication; Language recovery
  impairment, 50-56
  pathology, 104
  rehabilitation, 21
  therapy, 31, 32, 43-44, 53, 54, 84, 119, 145
Strabismus, 20
Stroke, left side, 2
Structure, classroom need, 67-68
Student "buddies," 71
Suicide, 130-131
Supervision, school, 71-72
Swallowing, rehabilitation, 44
Swallowing dysfunction. See
    Dysphagia
Swelling, brain, 10-12. See Also
    Edema

Teacher direction, specificity, 68
Teacher expectations, 70
Teacher preparation, 113-114
  & family, 115-116
  memory evaluation, 115
  reteaching vs. new learning, 114-116
Teasing, 71
Technology, assistive, 126
Temporal lobe, 3
  & blunt trauma, 3
  focal left damage, 59
  & psychiatric impairment, 59
  psychosis, 59
Testing. See *Assessment*

Test-retest effect, 104
Tests, classroom, 70
Tissue impairment, focal, 12
Tower of Hanoi, 50
Toxicity, medication, 18
Tracheostomy, 8
  & language deficit, 51
  & rehabilitation, 38-39
Trauma
  pedestrian, 2
  temporal lobe, 3
  vehicular, 2, 15, 19
Treatment plan, CT scan, 9
Tremors, 44
  intention, 40-41
Tutoring, hospital, 69

Unconsciousness. See *coma*
Unconventionality, 59

Vehicle accidents, 48
Vehicular injury, 29-30
Vehicular trauma, 25-26
Ventricular enlargement, MRI, 47
Verbal assessment, 50
Verbal fluency deficits, 49
Verbal recall, 47
Verbosity, 51, 59
Vertigo, postconcussion, 59
Visual cortex, 3
Visual memory, 47
Visuomotor, assessment, 45
Visuomotor deficits, 49
Visuoperceptual deficits, 48-49
Visuospatial, assessment, 45
Visuospatial deficits, 49
Visuospatial recall, 47
Voluntary movement, 2
Voluntary regulation, 4

Walkers, 44
Wired jaw, & language deficit, 51
Wisconsin Card Sorting Test, 49-50

Year-round educational
    programming, 86